Ministry and the Media

Also by Wesley Carr and published by SPCK:

The Priestlike Task (1985)

Brief Encounters: Pastoral Ministry through the Occasional Offices (1985)

The Pastor as Theologian: The Integration of Pastoral Ministry, Theology and Discipleship (1989)

Ministry
and the Media

WESLEY CARR

First published in Great Britain 1990
SPCK
Holy Trinity Church
Marylebone Road
London NW1 4DU

British Library Cataloguing in Publication Data

Carr, Wesley *1941–*
Ministry and the media.
1. Society. Role of mass media. Christian viewpoints
I. Title
261.1

ISBN 0–281–04463–5

Typeset by Pioneer Associates, Perthshire
Printed in Great Britain by
Dotesios Printers Ltd, Trowbridge, Wiltshire

To
New College,
The University of Edinburgh,
with thanks for an Honorary Fellowship
connected with
The Project
on the Media and Theological Education

CONTENTS

Contents

PART III

PREFACE

Debate rages over the shape of ministries in the Churches and the training required by the authorized ministers and by Christians in every walk of life. The discussion, however, is vitiated because it largely begins (and usually ends) within the Churches and their traditions. Yet whatever form the Churches' ministries will take, since they are 'ministries' (i.e. 'services'), they can only be considered in terms of the way that the Churches and their contexts act upon each other.

But the moment we mention 'context' we are involved with the media. Life today is media-saturated. The vague word 'media', for all its inherent difficulties, best describes the general context in which the Churches in all parts of the world now work. The difficulty of defining the term is discussed early in the book. But this cannot allow us to avoid facing it.

'Ministry' is equally notorious. This book approaches the subject specifically from the perspective of theological education. This phrase, too, has wide reference. It may describe the pre-ordination training or the continuing ministerial education of authorized ministers. But it equally refers to the many opportunities for learning which are offered to the laity, as well as to that undercurrent of persistent study which goes on as people read, listen and talk about the meaning of the Christian faith and its application to their lives and to those of others.

This book, then, is about ministry and is, therefore, for all ministers, lay and ordained, as well as for those who are interested in and intrigued by the Churches' continuing activity. The subject is considered through the twin themes of theological education and the media. Each is so large that together they could become impossible to handle. Theological education, therefore, is chiefly discussed in terms of the training of men and women for ordination, but includes the wider range implied in the phrase. I hope that the issues examined and the stance commended may be seen as not restricted to the question of ordination training alone but in every aspect of the Churches' work of education.

This study originates from work done for the Project on the Media and Theological Education, which is based at New College, Edinburgh, and sponsored by the Jerusalem Trust. The Trust has been, and remains, generous in its support for what has proved to be a pioneering enterprise in Great Britain. It is a pleasure to be associated with Professor Duncan Forrester and his colleagues at New College, and in this small way to acknowledge the honour they have done me by electing me an Honorary Fellow.

The Project began because some people believed that there was negligible awareness in the Churches and among their ministers of the impact of the contemporary media on the forms of Christian belief and expression—especially theological thinking. As so often, the first thought was that the training of the ministers should be altered to take these new (at least to most people in the Churches) phenomena into account and that a scheme should be offered. At this point I was contacted. I am not an expert in the media, although I know a little about pre- and post-ordination theological education, especially in the Church of England. At about the same time negotiations were in hand with Duncan Forrester in Edinburgh.

The outcome has been that we have run parallel projects. That in Scotland focused at first on the media and their impact, the work being headed by Dr Christopher Arthur. In England, by contrast, we have considered the task of theological education and moved from that to thinking about the media. In this piece of action research I have been assisted by fifty-five colleages, first as students and subsequently as newly ordained ministers. Their names are listed at the end of this Preface, together with an acknowledgement of the help received in setting up the Project from the staff of a number of colleges and courses. They have all contributed more than they may realize to this book, although naturally I alone am responsible for what is written here. I would hope, however, that they would recognize much and be stimulated in their own ministries by some of the arguments and suggestions, especially now that they are themselves educators in their Churches.

The link between media and theology was unexplored when we started. The outcome so far has been to some extent unexpected. But that is the proper nature of a Project. The whole enterprise is now moving ahead for a further three years, from which it is expected that further publications will emerge.

Wesley Carr
Bristol Cathedral
November 1989

PARTICIPANTS IN THE PROJECT 1986–88

The Project was organized on an area basis, which is reflected in the way that the names are listed.

BRISTOL

Trinity College
Nicholas Baines
Steve Butler
Colin Paterson
Mark Rylands

Wesley College
Paul Arnold
John Beadle
Malcolm Jones
Timothy McQuiban
Patricia Stockton

CAMBRIDGE

Ridley Hall
Stuart Thomas
Albert Watson

Wesley House
Stuart Bell
Paul Dear
Andrew Lunn
Michael Wilkinson

Westcott House
Christopher Harrison

Westminster College
Cecil White

THE MIDLANDS

Oscott College
Paul Cummins
Nicholas Heap
Adrian Wilcock

St John's College, Nottingham
Angela Cooke
Peter Cornish
Alastair Cutting
Simon Gatenby
Pamela Hoyle
Michael Jeffries
Kendrick Richards
Michael Talbot
Christopher Woadden

DURHAM

Cranmer Hall
Nigel Anstey
Jonathan Chaffey
Janet Chapman
Mark Farr
Simon Gates
Jane Page
Susan Richardson

Participants in the project 1986–88

North East Ordination Course
Joan Dotchin
Irene Page
Ken Potter

Ushaw College
Andrew Browne
Michael Holmes
Christopher Hughes
Michael McCormick
Mark McManus
Barry O'Sullivan
Peter Stanton

MANCHESTER
Hartley Victoria College
Andrew Howorth
Pamela Pettitt
Paul Webb

Northern College
Wendy Baskett
Gloria David
Colin Foreman
Susan Henderson
Alan Kennedy
Ian Ring

Staff from the following institutions invited some of their students to take part (the person's name is that of either the then principal or the tutor involved):

BRISTOL
Wesley College   The Revd Dr W D Stacey
Trinity College   The Revd James Jones

CAMBRIDGE
Ridley Hall   The Revd John Mockford
Wesley House   The Revd David Deeks
Westcott House   The Revd Richard McKenna
Westminster College   The Revd Janet Sowerbutts

THE MIDLANDS
Oscott College   The Rt Revd Mgr Michael Kirkham
St John's College Nottingham   The Revd Gordon Oliver

DURHAM
Cranmer Hall   The Revd Michael Williams
The North East Ordination Course   The Revd Canon Dr Michael Kitchener
Ushaw College   The Revd Stephen Clayton

MANCHESTER
Hartley Victoria Methodist College   The Revd Graham Slater
Northern College   The Revd Dr R J McKelvey
Northern Baptist College   The Revd Dr Brian Haymes

In addition the Southern Dioceses Ministerial Training Scheme (The Revd John Goodall) was eager to participate, but it proved impossible to fit students from there into my schedule.

Part One

INTRODUCTION

In this section we shall begin by exploring what we are talking about when we speak of 'the media'. The term notoriously defies precise definition. This, however, is not a consequence of intellectual laziness or lack of attention to the question. The problem lies in the nature of those phenomena which we generally call 'media'.

The first chapter sets the scene within which the argument of this book takes place. It illustrates uses of the word 'media' and shows some of the ways in which they function. A few preliminary connections are also made with theological education.

In the second chapter the concept of 'interpretation' is introduced and it is suggested that this accurately describes the nature of contemporary ministry. Whether preaching a sermon, writing an article for a newspaper, hearing a confession or counselling someone in distress, ministers (whether lay or ordained) are being invited to interpret a facet of human life in the light of the Christian gospel which they represent. For such a ministry, a clear sense of the process that is happening, of the content in the encounter and of the context in which it is taking place is essential. Process, content and context are today all affected by the media-saturated environment.

Finally in Part I some thoughts are presented on the specific problem of how we communicate religious ideas. How can an amalgam of feeling and understanding, tradition and present belief, ever be articulated? And, even if it can, how might the result be communicated to someone else? The rise of communications' studies in recent years has exposed the enormity of what is being attempted. While there is no need to surrender to despair in the face of this, theological students and ministers now need a clearer idea of what they are about.

1 WHY BOTHER WITH THE MEDIA?

In most institutions the maxim at times of major change is: 'When in doubt, change the training.' Education can be blamed for the inadequacies of people's ability to cope with unforeseen demands, and used to sustain vague hopes of a new world. This is certainly the case among Christians, who persist in the illusion that ministers, both lay and ordained, somehow ought to spring fully 'trained' from their courses.

Scarcely a month passes without a new report or directive being produced. The urban problems of the Churches have recently been given priority, especially in the Church of England. Now, as we begin to hear calls to examine the survival of the rural church, evangelism (in the shape of the proposed 'Decade of Evangelization') reappears. Underlying everything remain the prominent issues of the age, such as racism, sexism and feminism. Those who speak passionately on each issue seem to demand that, because of its key importance in contemporary life, it should be recognized as a determining influence in the design of every syllabus.

All such claims are in their way reasonable. But not surprisingly those responsible for the Churches' ministries tend to respond with increasing scepticism. Why should any single issue be assigned special, least of all dominant, status? What is more, why should any such contemporary notion (and possibly, therefore, passing fad) supplant the time-honoured and well tested themes? Indeed, faced with increasingly conservative students in Churches which seem also, at least in their public forums, to be tending towards similar conservatism, this response is implicitly strengthened. Might it not be better to eschew such modern trends and get back to basics—Bible, history, doctrine, ethics, and pastoralia?

It would be a rash person, therefore, who merely proposed

without much qualification that the media should be assigned priority in preparing tomorrow's ministers, lay and ordained. Why should the media be taken as the orienting factor? Why bother with them at all?

THE PERVASIVE MEDIA

In *Television and Religion*, William Fore tells this story:

> Not long ago a friend of mine arrived in New York City to take a job with the American Bible Society. He had come from Vancouver. Although he was a very media-wise person, the communication scene amazed him. 'Half the people in New York City are doing nothing all day but producing, moving, or working with information', he said. 'It's incredible!'

Fore goes on to say that he was speaking more accurately than he knew. More than half the American labour force is now 'involved in the production, dissemination, or use of information in its various forms. Almost half of the US gross national product is generated by information related activities.'[1]

This story indicates why the issue of the media is not a new one which has suddenly been discovered. If the task of theological education is to prepare men and women to be ministers both now and in the future, then the dimension represented by the media can no longer be ignored. It is already crucial. A few teachers may remember a time before television. No students, however, are today in that position. They, and those to whom increasingly the Church is seeking to convey its message, know no other world than one which is saturated with media, especially television.

Television effectively began shortly after the Second World War. In the UK the turning point is usually reckoned to have been the Coronation of Queen Elizabeth II in 1953. This event demonstrates the profound nature of the change. When George VI was crowned in 1937, the ceremony was broadcast on the radio. But while the king and queen received communion, the broadcasters cut away to sacred music. There was scarcely much change in attitude at the beginning of 1953. Controversy raged over what was sacred and how far to allow television to intrude. The Archbishop of Canterbury (Geoffrey Fisher) and the Prime Minister (Winston Churchill) both expressed reservations and wanted restrictions on the extent of coverage allowed to the BBC. The argument was resolved in favour of the full showing of the ceremony.[2] This was the moment when in Great Britain television's power was first publicly acknowledged. It was also for many their first personal encounter with 'the box'.

Since then the pervasive spread of television has been startling. In 1955 just over one third of households in the United Kingdom possessed a television; by 1960 eight out of ten had a set; and by the mid-1970s nine in ten households had at least one set, with more and more having more than one.[3] It is now a widespread assumption that a message on television will reach virtually the whole population of the United Kingdom. The same is true in much of the rest of the world, especially continental Europe, Japan and the United States. Even if a message does not in practice reach every person, it will come nearer to such an achievement through television than through any other medium. In one generation it has become the dominant means of communication.

It is easy to give 'shock' figures. For example, on an average day in the United Kingdom about thirty-eight million people watch television, usually for about two to three hours;

The ordinary American child by the age of eighteen will have watched more hours of television commercials than an undergraduate will spend in class during a four-year university education. There is no reason to doubt that similar figures apply in other countries where television is developed.

A working man spends more time watching television than doing anything else, except working and sleeping.[4]

Studies have also computed the amount of sex and violence, the range of attempted persuasion in advertising, and the hidden bias in news and documentaries. Others can argue the case for regulation or deregulation of television. Leaders of different religions become concerned about its potentially 'corrupting' effect upon the beliefs of their adherents. Christians in the mainline Churches become anxious about the electronic church which has emerged in the United States and whether it is fundamentally reshaping the gospel so that people, other than the manipulated, will become incapable of believing anything.

These are the sorts of issues about which protest develops and campaigns are launched.

In terms of the future this medium is also profoundly significant.

> After parents and before school, television is the primary educator of our children. It has become a dominant voice in our lives and a major agent of socialization in the lives of our children.[5]

Many people express concern over the apparent passivity of today's young people, who have been brought up in a new world in which television is a normal, not a special, feature. These questions, it should be noted, whatever their importance, tend to be posed by pre-television people, those whose assumptive world is different from that of the children they are discussing. It may be, for instance, that just as a war generation seems to have built up certain defences against having to cope with the pressures of bombs, evacuation and general deprivation, so a generation rich in images on the television and sounds on the radio may be more defended against them than others may be able to recognize.

There is, however, another side to the mass media. For example, lonely people may find some companionship from the radio and television. Such a function may become increasingly important in a society where the population overall is ageing. Others discover in the public figures a sense of stability and security in a world which appears to be disintegrating. Again, this may not be wholly desirable as they develop their fantasies and lose touch with reality. But having some such 'person' to whom to cling may at a superficial level enable some people to survive in a world which feels increasingly unfriendly.

More than this there is a wide range of people for whom the mass media are a major means of instruction. News and documentary programmes can be both entertaining and illuminating. We see, indeed now expect to see, parts of our world, our universe and ourselves, which our predecessors did not. This is obviously the case with explorations of nature and of art. But it is also true of social exchange. We have already noted the importance of the Coronation in 1953 as a turning point in the British people's awareness of the mass media. It may on reflection also have been a moment of change in their self-awareness as citizens.

In October 1952 Churchill argued that 'modern mechanical

arrangements' could be allowed into Westminster Abbey to enable people to see what the general public might see but not what would only be seen by 'high ecclesiastical dignitaries and state functionaries . . . whose duties require them to be close to the Sovereign'.[6] Such thinking is now inconceivable. The extended family of viewers to which people can believe that they belong may not only enrich their lives by fantasy; it may also be having significant impact on the concept of the individual within society. The implied contact between citizens and their leaders, which the seductive intimacy of television generates, may be changing our sense of relationship and connections within social hierarchies. And when we leave these grand speculations there remains the not unimportant point in our modern pressured world that television gives people permission to relax.

THE MEDIA AS 'CHURCH'

But these areas of popular discussion about the impact of television are peripheral issues compared with the main reasons why the media are so significant. The mass media, notably television, are now a major factor in ritual and rites. In other words, they do not have an effect upon the Churches and religion; rather, they appear to occupy the same space in people's lives and in the shape of society. James Curran has suggested that 'the modern mass media in Britain now perform many of the integrative functions of the Church in the middle ages'.[7] Peter Horsfield, speaking about Australia, comments that

> television needs to be seriously considered as an operative religious faith for a large proportion of the population. The actual figures are that for four and a half months of twelve hour days people are watching. The quasi-religious aspect of television (as of all the mass media) needs noticing by those responsible for the life of the church and the training of its ministers.[8]

These media link people with one another and emphasize collective values in a society. For example, in Great Britain the media promote the monarchy as a symbol of collective identity as the Church once did. Curran, however, invites us to go further. He suggests that the modern media

> have also given, at different times, massive and disproportionate attention to a series of 'outsiders'—youth gangs, muggers, squatters,

drug addicts, student radicals, trade union militants—who have tended to be represented as powerful and irrational threats to 'decent society'.[9]

These identifications lead to witch hunts, and moral panics are reinforced. So he concludes, 'The mass media have now assumed the role of the church in a more secular age of interpreting and making sense of the world to the mass public.'

The important point about this quotation is not whether Curran is right that the mass media are replacing (or even have replaced) the Church but that from his perspective he can make the comparison at all. Occasionally, when confronted by the overwhelming new technologies of communication, we may be tempted to think that they have somehow created a niche in society and filled it. Curran, however, with others, shows that the media occupy a place which has been and remains of continuing significance in a society. That space is where rite and ritual are expressed and embodied. In other words, for the Churches, which have historically performed this task, the media by their existence raise the question of the continuing public significance of religion and specifically of the Christian faith. The media, therefore are more significant for the Church than its members and leaders may immediately realize.

There is also a second area of reflection which arises from this comparison. The significance of the mass media goes beyond that range of moral and social questions that customarily concern the Churches. They raise issues about the structures of a society and hence about the ways in which culture is transmitted. They thus directly compete (or appear to compete) with the Churches for significance in an area which the Churches aspire to influence.[10]

Churchpeople generally overlook this. It is, for example, interesting to observe the similarity of the debates in the Churches from 1950 onwards, when faced with the prospect of independent television, to those in the late 1980s when faced with deregulation and the arrival of satellite broadcasting. On both occasions the argument concerned standards and questions of the moral good of society. There were protests about the malign influence of the media and gentle interpretations of the way in which the media were believed to impinge on aspects of communal life.

But these are easily dealt with and eventually, after the initial period of anxiety, can be assigned the limited importance that they deserve in discussion of political and social action. The painful significance of the modern mass media for the Churches — and, hence, the reason why they must be taken into account in any contemporary programme of theological education — is greater. On the one hand we can perceive the areas of personal life which they affect; but on the other hand, and of no less importance, we can note how they affect the cultural setting in interaction with which we each live.

THE CULTURAL POWER OF THE MEDIA

The modern mass media, which now primarily means television, perform three distinctively significant and discernible tasks.

First, they are shaping the notion of the world by which people live and orient themselves. Neil Postman gives a neat, if sad, illustration from one extreme group. The Amish live in Pennsylvania in as much isolation from American culture as they can manage. They are specifically forbidden to watch films or television, but it seems that they can be employed in films. When the film *Witness* was being made in 1984, the star was Harrison Ford. The Church elders warned their flock not to interfere with the film crews, but apparently several people, when their day's work was done, went to watch.

> 'We read about the movie in the paper', said an Amish woman. 'The kids even cut out Harrison Ford's picture.' She added: 'But it doesn't really matter to them. Somebody told us he was in *Star Wars* but that doesn't mean anything to us.' The last time a similar conclusion was drawn was when the executive director of the American Association of Blacksmiths remarked that he had read about the automobile but that he was convinced it would have no consequences for the future of his organization.[11]

This is an idiosyncratic example, but it reminds us of the obvious point that there is now nothing that does not find at least some of its expression through television. People, aspects of society, or every point of public interest, political, educational, religious, sporting, scientific, whatever aspect of life we consider, all are mediated through television. We may, then, see television as 'the command centre of the new epistemology',[12] through which public understanding of everything is eventually given much, if not all, of its shape. Although we may from time to time hear dissent from this proposition, even the terms of that dissent seem to be determined by the fact of the mass media and the agenda that they set. For the medium purports to report and present, but on reflection we discover that it also creates and manipulates.[13] The world, therefore, which we now inhabit is largely shaped by the mass media.

Second, the mass media—again chiefly television—become the place where values are embodied. This is a genuinely religious area. Gregor Goethals has argued that television offers a secular iconography of technology, which contrasts with the traditional sacred icons.

> The heroes and heroines in the sacred icons were portrayed as exceptional human beings, though morally frail; their image witnessed a faith in a divine, transcendant being. The icons of technology, by contrast, portray a gospel that can deliver people from ugliness, age, even death and destruction. Central to the new faith is the belief that human nature is not constant and that people like products can continually be changed, updated, improved and packaged.[14]

At the core of this new faith is the entertainment milieu, by which the value of everything is implicitly assessed. Postman's book is full of illustrations of this. He sums up the situation thus:

> It's great to be an entertainer. Indeed, in America God favours all those who possess both a talent and a format to amuse, whether they be preachers, athletes, entrepreneurs, politicians, teachers or journalists. In America, the least amusing people are its professional entertainers.[15]

Allowing for exaggeration and the distinctive complexity of American culture, he and other commentators have, however, hit on a key issue. The mass media do not just bring a range of possible 'faiths' to the viewers, listeners and readers. If that were all, people would merely choose from the goods offered. But in fact they have transformed both the way in which people believe, and hence, so it begins to seem, their capacity to believe.

> As the entertainment milieu trains people to believe tentatively and with elasticity . . . the very concept of faith—to believe in that which you cannot see and cannot understand—comes with difficulty.[16]

Thirdly, we may note that the media now seem to express the essence of contemporary culture in a way in which hitherto other symbol-bearing institutions, including the Church, have done. These functions used to be spread throughout a society. As, however, plural forms of society have developed, so has the centralizing function of the media (especially television) increasingly emerged to hold the prevailing cultural norms. In the USA, for example, it might be suggested that the cycle of natural rhythms of the seasons and religious festivals has had to yield to those sports seasons which are assigned a dominant place in the media programme.[17]

But this is not purely an American curiosity. A similar tendency may be observed in Great Britain. Where television is prominent, national events such as a presidential election or a royal wedding are turned into television rituals in which by viewing virtually the whole nation shares. Katz and Dayan have suggested that by not being there but participating through the medium of television, people go through a ritual reliving of national myths. Few, for instance, can take part in a spectacular space voyage. But by 'being there' through television coverage, the pioneering aspect of the American self is reaffirmed.[18] The media, therefore, are firmly set now in the context of ritual, that is, those mechanisms by which individuals and communities manage change and especially transition. This question has been widely discussed by pastoral theologians in the context of religion and religious institutions and their place within a society. Now, however, we need to think more widely in terms of the prevailing culture as a whole.[19]

The cultural power of the media is a central issue today. The spirit of a culture may decline in two main ways. One, the Orwellian, transforms culture into a prison. In the other, the Huxleyan culture is turned into a burlesque:

> What Huxley teaches is that in the age of advanced technology, spiritual devastation is more likely to come from an enemy with a smiling face than from one whose countenance exudes suspicion and hate. In the Huxleyan prophecy, Big Brother does not watch us, by his choice. We watch him, by ours.[20]

The issue is not, however, as simple as this. There is today a major debate about the cultural power of the new media, and it inevitably remains unresolved. Media studies themselves began prior to the Second World War, working on the popular assumption that broadcasting and film could and did sway people's opinions and indeed votes. This belief—for that is what it was—seemed to be confirmed by the rhetorical power of Goebbels and Hitler and the radio oratory of Churchill. To some degree that belief persists. Since the war, however, studies have suggested that matters are more complex. We entered a period when attempts were made to measure effect, but always with disrupted results. While, for instance, people felt that the new prevalence of the mass media must carry some direct effects, no study seemed incontrovertibly to demonstrate these. Violence and sex, in particular their linking in pornography, were the main focus of attention. But while the 'feeling' remained strong that the media were affecting people, we seemed unable to determine what gave rise to such a belief. Now in media studies the concept of a powerful medium which creates a culture is questioned and research is shifting to examine how audiences participate interactively with the media.

The field remains controversial, but certain tendencies may be discerned. Some focus on socio-political interests or class differences in the audience. Others draw on semiotics and the polysemy of the television text.* Drawing these, and other perspectives, together, Fiske concludes:

> In a mass society the materials and meaning systems out of which cultures are made will almost inevitably be produced by the culture industries; but the making of these materials into culture, that is, into the meanings of self and of social relations, and the exchange of these materials for pleasure is a process that can only be performed by their consumer-users, not by their producers.[21]

But whatever the newest discovery, the crucial point for the Church is that the media are now the major cultural phenomenon. They shape the world in which people live; they embody for many, if not most, the values by which they live; and they express the essence of contemporary culture and have become primary ritual bearers within it.

---

*   These two terms are probably unfamiliar to many readers. 'Semiotics' is the study of patterned human behaviour in every mode. 'Polysemy' is used of words and the way in which they may have more than one meaning.

ALTERED CAPACITIES AND THE MEDIA

These media, as a cultural phenomenon, do not merely constitute an interest in society; their role within it is more profound. We should, however, note a further effect. Their existence affects people's capacity to receive information and signals. In other words, it is important to note the fact of the media as media: i.e. something interposed between object and subject which transmits data. Television in particular has extended the human sensory apparatus. Until this century most human beings have lived with the inbuilt limitations of their biology. The eye can only see so far, the ear hear so much, and so on. Inventions such as the telescope and the hearing-aid have only slightly extended the range. We perceive a relationship between the capacity of the eye and ear and what is offered to it, together, we suspect, with the capacity of the brain to process such information.

We touch here significant questions about art and music. Such processing is not merely taking the data and giving them shape; it is also absorbing the effect of seeing and processing those data into a world view which is suffused with information and with values, discernments and decisions. When, however, we increase the information by extending the 'receiver', the internal capacity to interpret must be seriously affected. It is obviously difficult at present to know precisely how and to what extent. Nevertheless we are faced with a question for theology, as well as other disciplines: are human beings changing (or being changed) fundamentally?

Secondly, the modern mass media alter the balance between the different senses. Teachers of children have long spoken of the 'eye-gate' and the 'ear-gate' and the different facility of each. Newspaper editors have known that one picture is worth a thousand words. But the impact of television gives such priority to the eye and what is seen that other means of perception seem to be correspondingly diminished. Hearing, even smelling and touching, may decline. But that is not all. Our internal means of discerning what is real from what is unreal may equally be affected.

We may illustrate this from the reporting of a recent disaster. When in December 1988 the Pan-Am jumbo jet crashed in Scotland, television and radio gave the event immediate coverage. Quickly the newsrooms expanded their range, mixing pictures with speculation, opinion and pressing people to premature judgement. At an early stage in the chaos and uncertainty, the newscaster referred viewers back to the scene in a suitably serious and personal fashion: 'Any more news, John?' The reporter on the spot replied: 'I'm afraid there are no new pictures. Back to the studio.' Implicit in this fragment of everyday television is the assumption that there is only one genuine sensory means of learning about the disaster—the eye. We can sympathize with the reporter and producer. In the situation there was little else they could do: the viewers' (note the description) expectation of pictures leads those responsible for what is primarily a visual medium to confine their thinking to visual terms. But at the same time, these are assumed to be the sole means whereby people can take in news, especially worrying news.

A third effect of these media is the way in which they influence our preferences. These may be aesthetic, but they are also social and structural, as well as economic. We have noted the cultural power of the media. This lies less in their ability to affect people who watch and listen than in their function in creating the assumptive world which all inhabit. Obviously there is the personal impact of this facet of the media. But this power is not restricted to that area. That is why we are mistaken if we seek in ourselves signs of direct influence or become preoccupied with this. We shall later note Television Awareness Training, which is designed to heighten personal awareness and inspire a corresponding sense of responsibility. There is much in its favour, but we should also recognize its limitations. Social impact, implicit colonialism, economic dominance come together to remind us that, when we today mention the media, we are speaking of the context and the content of every aspect of our lives.

THE MEDIA, LEISURE AND RELIGION

The notion of the 'media', therefore, is not just one among many influences on contemporary human life. We are now used to living in our pluralistic society with different ways of seeing things. Theologians, for example, have long been accustomed to reconciling their distinctive viewpoint with that of, say, the

15

Darwinian scientist or the astrophysicist. Gagarin's remark from his space capsule that he could not see God neither alarms the believer nor excites the unbeliever: it is irrelevant and naive. Different perspectives can be held together, and we have discovered that we can live with them. The Church, too, can and does survive and contribute to a world in which its message and interpretation of life's meaning is not the only, or even the most prominent, one. The mass media, however, are having a particular and different impact. For they both restructure the world which we inhabit and reorder our ability to realize what we perceive. In a sense, therefore, they now constitute the primary world which we inhabit and to which we contribute.

We can, therefore, begin to see the magnitude of the general effect of our culture being media-saturated. But although this might be of some importance to those thinking about ministry, we still have to establish why it is of such specific importance that sensitivity to the media should be the norm of training programmes. An unexpected, but useful, way into that issue is provided by considering leisure. This key area of human life is profoundly affected by the advent of the mass media. Leisure is not rest from work. It is better thought of as the time which a person or group has for choosing, as opposed to other times when they are subject to the demands of others. This definition draws attention to the complex nature of leisure. It is neither rest nor activity. It is one aspect of life in which the individual's sense of control and being controlled alters.[22] Historically, leisure in this sense has been the privilege of certain classes, especially philosophers and religious leaders.

It may not often feel like it, but ministers are people of leisure. Much of their life consists of 'choosing time' and they are accountable to themselves, and thence to God, for what they do with it. It is mainly during moments or periods of leisure that we reflect upon the dilemmas of existence with which religion is concerned. At a simple level these emerge in the family, where relations between the members raise moral and spiritual questions of love, trust, forgiveness, and, of course, their opposites. The assessment of life's priorities is usually a leisure activity. All these topics are also obvious facets of religion. Churchgoing, or any other form of religious practice, has become a private activity and so may be regarded in contemporary society as a use of leisure. The individual or family uses their choosing time to define the space within which they may reflect upon truth and meaning.

The link between such leisure and personal development is particularly illustrated during adolescence. Growing young people, who are struggling towards their own identity, learn the need for physical space in order to have energy to explore what we may call 'imaginative space'. This shows in the apparently permanent need for sleep and for the wide range of fantasy in which the growing adult indulges.

We need, however, to note how the mass media have encroached on both forms of 'choosing time', physical space and imaginative space. We shall discuss some of the possible effects later. But we have already observed from the few statistics quoted above the way in which this change is coming about.

The question for the Christian Church, therefore, is not whether the media should be given some attention. That would now seem unavoidable. Rather the issue is how to devise a way of living and ministering in this contemporary world, contributing to it, recognizing how it is affecting us, and above all learning how we are now to interpret the experiences of human life in the light of the gospel that we profess. We have already seen that there are some, like Avery Dulles, who think that the gospel itself has to be rethought because of the impact of the media on people's capacity to receive it. Such a possibility must be addressed if we are to produce ministers who can actually minister. As we shall see, there may be something in this view, especially if we are now producing, whether because of the media or not, a generation of people who lack historical awareness. Such questions are not easy to clarify or simple to resolve. But it is essential that they are faced, if the Church's ministers and people are to be anything more than marginal anachronisms in the twenty-first century.

By now, however, some may be counselling caution. It could be argued that the innate wisdom of centuries of civilization will not so easily surrender to media dominance. What is being described is essentially an American problem, which will only be partially European. Superficially this claim seems attractive. For example, it is undoubtedly true that the United States is in a different league as a society saturated by television. Many of the centres of the study of media and communication are in America and products of its film and television industries dominate the world market. Europeans, however, cannot escape so easily.

First, what happens in the United States tends to affect Europe, as well as the rest of the world. This will probably become increasingly obvious as the deregulation of radio and television progresses. The first programmes, for instance, on British satellite television (Sky Channel, February 1989, with four separate channels) have a distinctively American flavour. And so far as religion is concerned, there are already prospects of religious advertising on these new channels and it is more than probable that some American style religious programming will emerge. Trial series have already been filmed.[23]

Second, we should not underestimate the colonialism of the American media industry. Anyone who has travelled will probably have experienced somewhere in the world the incongruity of seeing old American programmes dubbed into local languages and shown with bizarre inappropriateness. But they are shown and watched, whatever the prevailing native culture. Colin Morris describes the Satellite Instructional Television Experiment in India in 1975. A satellite belonging to the United States Government was relocated to include India in its 'footprint'. One television set in over two thousand remote villages came to life, but each was watched by about two thousand people. Before this almost all of them had never seen a film or read a paper, and only about half had heard the radio.[24] We should not doubt the power of the media, and the power resides primarily in the US. Not only are many of the programmes created there, but also the models of management and production.

The issues that we are raising, therefore, while acutely observable in the United States, are not confined there. Nor is it merely a question of whether a new form of cultural imperialism will take over the world. Such serious matters need discussing, but they could scarcely be the most important questions for today's hard-pressed theological educators. But we can too easily be seduced into discussing the question of quantity rather than the more profound underlying issue: that of the nature of religious truth and how it is to be proclaimed in any culture.

The popular, or mass, media have always been a key source and stimulus to the religious imagination. In older societies they may be the oral telling and handing on of folk tales, myths and stories. Sometimes the means of transmission are folk dances or theatre. To a large extent today, however, they may be mass media experiences, which come to us through novels, film, music and especially television.

Robert White has illustrated this point from the unexpected source of the life of Ignatius of Loyola. His was a remarkable life. Starting as a career soldier and courtier to the king of Spain, he found himself as a result of his leg being shattered by a cannon shot spending time in enforced convalescence. He asked for some books on chivalry, but all he was offered were a life of Christ and some lives of the saints.

> During intervals in his reading his thoughts wandered back and forth between ideals of chivalry and the images of the lives of the saints. In the background of these motivating symbols was the model of chivalry that shaped the idealism of young men in sixteenth-century Spain and which was embodied in the popular novels of the day. In the foreground was the ideal of saints such as Francis of Assisi and Dominic which shaped the future course of Ignatius' life and led him to express chivalry in terms of prayer, penance, the desire to make a pilgrimage to Jerusalem and place himself completely at the service of Jesus, his Lord and King. The full significance of this initial revelation-faith experience became evident only with successive stages of his life, but one can detect in this conversion experience the imagery of his Spiritual Exercises and the organising imagery of the spirituality in the religious order he later founded. What is striking is the influence of the popular culture and the popular media of the age in shaping personal religious symbols.[25]

Ignatius' age and the available media are remote from ours. But this story is a forceful reminder of the significance both of leisure (choosing time) and of popular culture.

Christians sometimes dismiss the popular media as *merely* entertainment. The caricature vicar who mentions a television programme in a sermon only after an apology ('I don't usually watch television, but I just happened to see . . . ') may represent something more prevalent than his own embarrassment. There is a strong suggestion that the media do not merit serious attention. This is matched by the way in which leisure, especially in some traditions, is also assigned less value than work. But in the light both of our reflections on the modern mass media and the story of Ignatius we can now begin to see that much of human life (indeed an increasing amount) is taken up in leisure, and that entertainment is not a neutral or even necessarily malign activity. It is one way in which space for reflection is, at least in theory, generated.

CONCLUSION

From this angle we may now return to ministry. This is as great a problematic area as the mass media, but one which is similarly full of controversy, energy and change. A point of primary contact between the two is that religious institutions and their leaders are involved in the transmission of culture. The more specific question facing those training ministers is how to transmit Christian faith in any particular time and place. The general issue of communications has always lain at the heart of the nature of the gospel itself. Although it has sometimes been reduced merely to the acquisition of skills, the fundamental questioning has never wholly been lost. Profound theological issues, forms of teaching and learning, and matters of technique are integrated in the concept of 'communications'. Content and process come together, often in a seemingly overwhelming way. This produces that sense of exhaustion and anxiety lest there be no limit or end to the exploring.

These and similar difficulties were identified at a consultation in 1986 on 'The Cultural Power of the New Media: Implications for Theological Education'. True to form in such gatherings, the members were awed by the range of issues which they disturbed. The concluding remarks by two members of the faculty at Union Theological Seminary, William Kennedy and Donald Shriver, accurately summed up the concern which now faces all theological educators:

> What we were trying [in this consultation] to isolate for theological education was what kind of early warning systems can we help develop in the consciousness of our seminaries as they train pastors that will help us ask these questions about the nature of human beings, human society, the ways we relate to a transcendent God, all of those fundamental, theological parts of what we might call our message. How are we being reshaped by a major turn in the media, in the means of communication and the search for meaning in our society?[26]

It seems in the light of this opening discussion that for any Church that intends to remain effectively ministering and evangelizing in the contemporary world, the question, 'Why the media and theological education?', is no question. The two cannot continue apart, so long as we believe that the Christian Church has a significant task in our human societies.

Notes

1. William F. Fore, *Television and Religion* (Minneapolis, Augsburg Publishing, 1987), p. 176.

2. Kenneth M. Wolfe, *The Churches and the British Broadcasting Corporation, 1922–1956* (London, SCM Press, 1984), pp. 497ff.

3. David Morley and Brian Whitaker, eds, *The Press, Radio and Television* (London, Commedia, n.d.), p. 22.

4. Collected from various sources in C. J. Arthur, 'Television, Transcendence and Religious Education', *Farmington Occasional Paper 27* (Oxford, Farmington Institute for Christian Studies, 1987).

5. Jean Marie Hiesberger, 'The Ultimate Challenge to Religious Education', *Religious Education* 76 (1981), p. 357.

6. Wolfe, op. cit., p. 497.

7. James Curran, 'Communications, Power and Social Order', in Michael Gurevitch, Tony Bennett, James Curran and Janet Woollacott, eds, *Culture, Society and the Media* (London, Methuen, 1982).

8. Peter Horsfield, 'Religious Dimensions of Television's Uses and Content', *Colloquium* 17 (1985), p. 62.

9. Curran, op. cit.

10. See generally Bernice Martin, *A Sociology of Contemporary Cultural Change* (Oxford, Blackwell, 1981).

11. Neil Postman, *Amusing Ourselves to Death* (London, Methuen, 1986), p. 93, quoting from *The New York Times*, June 7, 1984.

12. Postman, op. cit., p. 79.

13. See Peter Conrad, *Television, the Medium, and its Manners* (London, Routledge & Kegan Paul, 1982).

14. Gregor Goethals, *The TV Ritual; Worship at the Video Altar* (Boston, Beacon Press, 1981), p. 84.

15. Postman, op. cit., p. 5.

16. Avery Dulles, 'The Church is Communications', US Catholic Documentary Service, 1971 (New York, US Catholic Conference).

17. Michael Real, *Mass Mediated Culture* (Englewood-Cliffs, Prentice-Hall, 1977), pp. 90ff.

18. Elihu Katz and Daniel Dayan, 'Media Events: On the Experience of Not Being There', *Religion* 15 (1983), p. 305.

19. See especially Victor Turner, *The Ritual Process* (London, Routledge & Kegan Paul, 1969).

20. Postman, op. cit., p. 160.

21. John Fiske, *Television Culture* (London, Methuen, 1987), p. 323.

22. See, e.g., Stanley Parker, *The Future of Work and Leisure*, (London, McGibbon & Kee, 1971), for an early work; and Charles Handy, *The Age of Unreason* (London, Hutchinson, 1989) for more recent evidence and prognostication.

23. Peter Elvy, *Buying Time* (Southend-on-Sea, McCrimmon, 1987).

24. Morris, op. cit., p. 63.

25. Robert A. White, 'Formation for Priestly Ministry in a Mass-Mediated Culture', *Seminarius* 4, p. 811.

26. Report of a Consultation at Union Theological Seminary, New York, October 29–31, 1986: *Cultural Power of the New Media: Implications for Theological Education*, p. 21.

2 AN INTERPRETATIVE MINISTRY

'Media' is an elastic word, which adjusts to fit whatever presuppositions anyone may bring to it. Because its definition is controversial and problematic, 'media' seems to pose a philosophical or linguistic conundrum rather than refer to a dimension of contemporary culture with which the Churches' ministers need to come to terms.

Most often 'the media' are television, radio and the press. Sometimes we add cinema, music and books. The distinctive thrust of the term, however,

> is to separate out as *different* and therefore worthy of distinctive kinds of study, those *means and processes* of communication which are *industrialized* and thus able to carry out 'messaging' activities on a large scale (via mass production and mass distribution).[1]

There is no 'pure' definition of 'media'. What they represent and their effect are only perceivable in interaction, whether between producer and consumer, broadcaster and viewer, or between institutions of control or ritual significance within a society. When we discuss 'media', we are in all these areas at the same time. The term is both obvious and bewildering.

If we are to work with common sense—we know, after all, roughly what we mean by the media—and with critical clarity, we need a different approach from one which proceeds from definition to application. Such a venture should not be unfamiliar to theologians who are accustomed to proceed through interaction with people, Scripture or tradition towards the temporary resting-places of hypothetical definitions. The participants in the Project, for example, followed a line which was consistent with their experience of learning as theological students. They carefully noted the term, trying always to avoid using 'media' casually. Whenever it arose in discussion they examined the implied content and overtones, in order to discover, as best they could, the presuppositions which they themselves were making. The usefulness of such an approach became clear as the work progressed. We shall, therefore, in this section adopt a similar stance. This allows us to make progress in our thinking without, however, having to base it upon controversial, disputable, and probably inadequate definitions.

We have already noticed some of the complexity of the impact of the mass media.

> As the mass media have developed they have incontrovertibly achieved two things. They have, between them, diverted time and attention from other activities and they have become a channel for reaching more people with more information than was available under 'pre-mass media' conditions.[2]

Denis McQuail goes on to point out that institutionally the media compete with other institutions. These in turn have to respond, either by adapting themselves or by trying to make use of the mass media for their own ends. A specific example of such struggles is the way in which the Churches in the United States have responded to television. Some have conformed, transforming their largely world-denying evangelicalism into a television-affirming 'gospel'—the so-called 'tele-evangelists'. Others, chiefly the mainline Churches, have been uncertain how to respond and, excluded from the networks (or perhaps excluding themselves), have turned extensively to study and training with media awareness.[3] Whatever the practical outcome of this divergence, the fact of it alone makes clear that even traditional Churches, which may have no wish or intention of much direct engagement with the media, have to take into account this institutional effect. For they are, whether they perceive it clearly or not, institutions within this society.

This instance directs us to the point of significance for Churches and ministers: how we are to perceive, to live with and usefully grasp what is happening to and through us in our interaction with and participation in our media-saturated culture. In other words, we are concerned with interpretation.

'INTERPRETATION' DEFINED

Interpretation is a critical issue of our age. Yet the word is itself difficult to define. In English it has two main senses: first, to make something clear or explicit, expounding a meaning; but second, to explain something to oneself. These have been conflated in our post-Freudian age and together provide the following description of what we are doing when we interpret: 'by explaining something to oneself, to create a way of seeing data which enables oneself and others jointly to discover a new meaning and create a new occasion for action'.[4]

We may contrast 'interpretation' with 'understanding'. 'Understanding' includes a sense of confidence which is increasingly felt to be misplaced. It implies correct knowledge that may be possessed, or perception that may be achieved. But contemporary human experience contradicts both these expectations. Living seems to consist more of a series of struggles and continual attempts at grasping sufficient awareness of ourselves, what is happening to us and our place within the world, to be able to take another step in life. This whole process is included in 'interpretation'. It is not that we deny the possibility of understanding; it is rather that while we wish it were possible, our experience tells us otherwise. Similarly this does not mean that there are no norms and that we are condemned to a relativistic stance. It is simply that the limitations of our human capacities are becoming more obvious to us, and we, especially those who think and may be expected to give guidance or a lead to others, are more acutely aware of them.

For those, therefore, whose task is to communicate the gospel to congregations, but even more to interested enquirers, and to develop people's spirituality, interpretation describes the form of all their activity. Ministers, like most religious people, have been accustomed to think in a naive sense of the word: the 'interpretation' of Scripture, for instance, or the 'interpretation' of tradition. In pastoral studies, however, we now begin to see that interpretation describes a general stance for ministers. It is not something that they do with Scripture, tradition or experience. It refers to the way in which in order to exercise ministry, they have to learn how to link their internal experience with the external world, so that those whom they encounter may, through them, discover access to the gospel as an interpretative dimension to their lives.[5] It follows, therefore, that in any scheme of Christian education interpretation must be central.

The media provide a distinctive, fascinating and potentially useful way of directing trainee ministers to this key component of their present learning and future ministry, as the student participants in the Project discovered. When we study ourselves and our context, using the mass media as a focus, we can neither escape with an academic detachment into theoretical questions nor avoid our internal experience, the feelings which are generated in us. From this process a series of key concepts emerges. Each offers insights into the nature of the world in which the Church now ministers as well as the vocation of the ministers themselves. Above all by using the concept of the media, as outlined above—a working notion rather than a fixed definition—we are able to clarify the complicated idea of 'interpretation'.

INFORMATION, SELECTION AND RELEVANCE

Interpretation, whatever its aim and the context in which it occurs, clearly requires some information with which the interpreter can work. This observation immediately locates us in today's world. For this is the age of information and information technology. The problem is no longer a shortage of information but an excess. People have to become adept at coping with the quantity of material that is hurled at them. They have to establish criteria according to which they allow it access to them, especially when so much is personally disturbing and emotionally draining. The old music hall gag, 'I don't wish to know that; kindly leave the stage', has become a sort of slogan for contemporary survival.

The issue, therefore, for the would-be interpreter is twofold: first, how to work with people who are increasingly adept at screening out unwanted data and are therefore becoming skilled at selective hearing and seeing; and second, how to establish a criterion of relevance.

There seems to be some evidence that people may be becoming more competent at defending themselves against having to deal with all data thrown at them. People who are swamped by the information overload of today's media-saturated world, may unconsciously be becoming skilled at defending themselves against too much intrusion. They allow only selected information to affect them. The consequences for a minister who wishes to interpret life using data from the gospel tradition are obvious: Which immediate data from experience do we select? What is being denied by such selection? How much can the selection be a shared process? and What gospel data can be admitted and employed?

Turning to the criterion of relevance, we first note that interpretation is a dynamic activity. Notions of data, material or information may sometimes be contrasted with the dynamic aspect. This is the familiar argument about the relationship between 'content' and 'process'. In a world which is overwhelmed with information, whatever its quality, anyone working with others towards an interpretation of life must incorporate the relevant data into their shared thinking. The word 'relevant' is notably problematic. But behind its use we may discern three clarifications.

'Relevance' first implies that useable data consist of immediate information. Interpretation is always an activity in the present tense. It occurs at a specific moment, even if what is being interpreted is past experience or even future expectation. So much is obvious and this idea of 'relevance' is easily grasped. But on reflection we may discern that the modern media are affecting the notion of 'immediate'. There seems decreasingly to be what we might call 'space in the moment'. The statistics are familiar: the average length of shot in a soap opera is about 5.4 seconds and possibly decreasing; when watching television viewers 'zap' (change channels through a hand-held signaller) every few seconds. The sense of the present moment of existence, therefore, is being altered, even if the consequences of this observation are as yet unclear. The media may be changing the concept of the present, and interpretation is essentially an activity of the moment.

Secondly, the notion of relevance implies that any interpretation must be comprehensible. It is no interpretation if, whether because of complicated content or extensive process, it remains with the interpreter alone and so beyond people's ability to grasp and use it. We shall later examine the apparent effect of the modern media on people's capacity for imagination, the faculty which is central for pastoral and evangelistic interpretation. The fact, however, that relevance includes comprehensibility reminds us that all communication functions in two directions: both transmission and feedback. If either is missing there is no communication. It seems possible that the existence of the modern media may be bringing about a shift in the capacity to imagine. If so, there will be a commensurate change in the nature of the comprehensible information. This is not solely a matter of intellectual grasp. The mind may be overwhelmed by data and find the criterion for relevance a conundrum. But there is also the problem of emotional capacity to cope, which, if it is distressed, seems to lead to a draining of the person and to issue in some form of apathy.

Thirdly, the concept of 'relevance' reminds us that communication includes consequences. Something is not relevant unless it can be grasped and seen to have an effect. In other words, we have to include in the notion of interpretation some idea of what might be the outcome of acquiring and absorbing new information. This dimension to interpretation is also changed by the existence of the modern media. It directs us to the question of memory and the way in which our behaviour changes according to what it has recalled from our memory. But if, as seems possible, what we mean by 'memory' is itself being altered by contemporary information technology, one part of which is the mass media, then this dimension to relevance is also in question.

The connection between theological learning and these questions of the quantity of information and the criterion of relevance is easily made. Selection is a point of major controversy in dealing with two thousand years of accumulated data and a range of disciplines. Many, if not most, students report a sense of being faced with an overwhelming amount of information. Many also claim that the criterion of relevance, in all three senses listed above, is not examined in their training. One result is that, despite the intentions of the educators, trainee ministers treat courses eclectically. In so doing they show themselves products of their age; they acquire skills in defending themselves against information overload.

In practice they are not very successful. As soon as they begin their public ministry many either shed much of what they have acquired or create a style of activity which is unsubtle—i.e. they believe that they should simply provide people with as much 'information' as possible. Behind these options lie two

contemporary attitudes to ministry which are equally unsophisti-
cated: one represents a type of 'pastoral concern', which mostly
lacks theological content; the other is 'a teaching ministry',
which issues in dilettantish courses and sermon series as the
minister's chief *raison d'être.*

One issue, therefore, which attention to the media illuminates
is the pressure to create an information overload. This, however,
now emerges from a different direction. Hitherto it has been
mainly considered to be the result of competing demands within
the Churches for pieces of specific content within the training
programmes. We can now see it as one effect of the media age, in
which people expect information but also learn how to ignore it,
and this attitude is itself a function of the prevailing culture.

INTERPRETATION AND A COMMUNITY OF THOUGHT

In order to be able to offer interpretation—i.e. to practise
ministry—we need to be able to assume a community of thought
among all involved. The media significantly contribute to this
notion at two levels. In the first place there is their global
perspective. The universal—that is, around the world—spread
of material is especially notable in the case of television. Secondly,
there is a corresponding local attitude which assumes shared
approaches and presumes intimacy. The collocation of these two
dimensions seems important when we think of the emotional
context in which interpretation is attempted.

The first point—the universal spread of material—has been
widely noted. Much output for television, for example, is
explicitly designed to be shown across the world. The series of
advertisements for Coca Cola are classics of this genre. The
words can be translated into any language without having to
alter the visual images. It seems likely that this tendency will
increase with the advent of satellite broadcasting.

Whether the dissemination of such programmes will destroy
local cultures or whether they will survive this onslaught remains
an open question. The second point, however, is more interesting.
The media operate on a basis of presumed intimacy. The press,
most clearly in the case of the proliferating free local papers,
models itself on broadcasting and adopts a similar style.
Whatever the medium, the presenters enter the home as 'one of
us'. They are considered friends and companions. But this

attitude encourages the easy assumption that 'we' all agree. Even the feedback programmes, which apparently encourage expression of disagreement, largely treat discussion as 'in the family'. Students on training courses on radio and television presentation are taught about this: 'Think of an individual and speak to him/her', or 'Think of one person and write with him/her in mind.'

This may be a useful practical skill. But underlying the stance is a significant further aspect. The illusion of universality or community of thought that is generated by the existence of the media makes it difficult to deal with anything specific. This may seem paradoxical when we consider the amount of material that the media absorb. The output at first sight looks like nothing but specific instances: stories, anecdotes, dramas, etc. But underlying all lies the presumption of a community of thought. This first categorizes the listener or viewer and by so doing diminishes their individuality.

We can illustrate this by thinking of a local church, which does something unusual. Here is a highly specific story. It might be compared and contrasted with similar stories from other churches. Nevertheless it possesses its own individuality, not least as far as the participants are concerned. When picked up by the media, however, it is likely to be implicitly categorized, perhaps as 'Church' or even 'Christian'. That in turn, however, is too small a managing category, and it is further subsumed under 'Religion'. So, by the time something is transmitted or published, the specific local story may have been re-located within the media's universal world. Because of this change of context it may lose its specificity. This process may contribute to some of the felt, but unfocused, discontent which Churches and clergy express about media presentations of church activity. What is to them intensely personal and locally expressed, seems to be diminished by being placed in the categories of the media but presented on the basis of presumed intimacy.

In the process of interpretation something highly specific is taken and, without being diminished, is set in a larger context. People are thus assisted to draw from it hitherto unperceived depths. The preacher, for example, does this with a text or with the gospel; a pastor does it with a fragment of human experience. They take the particular point, examine it with others and discern through that exercise a new context. Reflection on this may produce a different vision and so issue in an unexpected activity. What is particular is thus enlarged or universalized. The media sometimes seem to function in this way as they interpret life and the world in which it is lived. But by their nature they cannot in fact affirm anything specific because, in order to function, they have to sustain an illusion of a community of thought—their audience.

If, then, such an illusion has become, or is becoming, a given fact of contemporary life, it poses a question to the Christian Churches and their ministers about the style of interpretative activity that is now possible. Some of the difficulties experienced today with traditional forms of interpretation, preaching in particular, may be more to do with this issue than with the more familiar discussions about people's attention span and the need for visual impact. There is an acute problem of how we can place ourselves and our neighbours in a context which is neither one of spurious intimacy nor so global that we cannot apply it to ourselves. It may be that the present-day tendency towards the privatizing of religious life is one instinctive response to the need to manage this dilemma by finding a usable place for oneself between cloying intimacy and an incomprehensible universe.

IMITATION

So far we have considered two factors on which the media have an effect: the notion of understanding and the assumed community of thought. Now we turn to consider two points at which the media affect the sense of the self with which people operate: mimicry and historical continuity.

Anyone watching television, listening to the radio or reading the newspapers cannot fail to notice the amount of mimicry. People, both in regular programmes (especially soap opera) and advertisements, are promoted as models to be copied. It is assumed that many would wish to be like them. Television and the popular press imitate each other in style and feed off each other for content. There seems to be an inexhaustible supply of impersonators on television, who imitate one another. All this is entertaining. But there are two serious points that are worth noting: first, although clever mimicry can be a form of interpretation, mimicry is generally straightforward re-presentation; second, the notion of imitation is profoundly important in Christian faith, especially its spirituality.

The interpretation of life in the light of the Christian gospel is an interactive exercise. There is no compulsion to believe the gospel, only an invitation. This fact sustains the innovative power of the Christian faith: every situation is an opportunity for the generation of something new. Any suggestion, therefore, that an interpretation of life may come about through mimicry implicitly diminishes the gospel. The hearer may be invited to imitate Christ or the presenter. But copying, trying to emulate another without any genuine engagement with him or her, escapes interaction. Something essential to the gospel itself is lost.

Yet if a prevailing thrust within the cultural environment promotes mimicry, a series of key issues is raised for any Christian interpretation of life. Among these we may note, first, that this tendency may affect people's capacity to interact with one other more than is generally realized. If they are occupied with imitation, they are also going to be caught up in some form of emulation, with a consequent diminution of their ability to relate effectively as human beings, minister and people, counsellor and counselled. Second, the struggle for interpretation may be reduced in principle to the simple message: 'Be like me', or 'Do what I say'. In this way the minister is seduced into a directive attitude and the inevitable dependence upon him or her is intensified. It is not likely that spiritual or human growth will be enhanced on this basis. Third, more positively, the connection between the style of presentation and the content of what is being presented is highlighted as a perennial issue to be considered by anyone who would be a communicator. We shall return to this last point below.

A second major point, however, is more crucial. The theme of imitation is central to Christianity. The *imitatio Christi* as a primary form of the spiritual life is universally approved. What is more, spirituality as a topic is today being given increased attention. It is, for example, an area of concern in theological education, with a widespread feeling that contact with this dimension of the life of the individual and of the programme of training is easily lost.

Spirituality, whatever exactly we mean by it, is widely

acknowledged as including some idea of following or copying Christ. Yet if the notion of imitation is diminished to that of mimicry, then this central theme of the Christian life is deeply influenced by the environment in which learning about it occurs and ministry is exercised. Once more, therefore, we find something more than merely an effect from the media on an aspect of Christian life and learning. We discover that an aspect of the media-saturated world in which we now live is not impinging on Christianity at the periphery but is influential at its core. If spirituality which leads to discernment is proposed as the basis for Christian existence in a media-dominated world, we shall need to take more account of the questioning of spiritual stances that this promotion of mimicry implies.

A SENSE OF PLACE

The second area of discussion on personal identity concerns one's sense of place in history and how this is affected when past and present are confused. When trying to convey information, radio and television producers have to set a scene. They are, therefore, subject to a twofold pressure. On the one hand, they need to provide every event with a visual or aural context. On the other hand, their predecessors have already selected material for the previous output and this is the chief resource available. As a result, they tend to redefine the context for the new information in the limited terms of existing material. A familiar instance occurs in news broadcasts, when the words 'Library pictures' are flashed on the screen.

The miners' strike in 1985 offered an example of the confusion that these pressures may inadvertently induce in people. During reflective programmes, especially on the radio, presenters attempted to set the strike in a long historical perspective. But this wish to be helpful to the audience made it difficult for us to discover where we were. Were we hearing about the General Strike of 1926, the nationalization debate in 1947, the crisis of 1985, or about some underlying 'miners' activity' that surfaced at random from time to time? The problem was exacerbated on radio because there was less fluctuation of quality than there would be (at least at the moment) on television. The words, content and language, and songs sounded the same from whichever period they derived. The hearers were on reflection disconcerted because they were caught up in a redefining of the experience of history.

The issue of personal identity lies at the heart of any doctrine of human personality and hence of the incarnation. In the light of the effect of the mass media upon our experienced perception of time, it must now include attention to the question, *'When* am I?'. The interrelation of past, present and future is a key theme in theological endeavour. For example, the doctrine and the experience of the Eucharist involve a subtle reorienting of people's lives in relation to these three dimensions. When, however, each period, past, present or future, itself becomes obscured in the way described, then their interrelation may become too complex a problem to explore, at least in the familiar categories.

An instance of this happening occurred in the controversies over the Bishop of Durham's view on the resurrection. The argument may not, as seems to have been widely assumed, have its roots in a confrontation between traditional religious thinking and scientific secularism. On the contrary, the doctrine of the resurrection is obviously concerned with the interrelation of past, present and future. The subtleties of such a doctrine may then become progressively inaccessible at any level, because those three temporal aspects of life are becoming confused in our experience. The consequence is that none of them is comprehensible separately, and we are unsure how or where to begin an exploration of the relations between them.

This outcome cannot be blamed upon the media. But it is an intriguing instance of the effect of the fact of the existence of mass media rather than of anything that they explicitly present or seem to promote. It is, therefore, also an effect over which those working in them cannot be invited to assume control. We have, then, a further instance of the givenness of the new environment within which theology has to be pursued and ministry exercised.

THE MEDIA AND THE STRUCTURE
OF INTERPRETATION

We now turn to consider the structure of an interpretation. Here, too, the media-saturated age has its impact. For while interpretations are necessarily temporary, and therefore fragmentary and incomplete, the media seem to make any interpretation distinctively complete.

Interpreting is a dynamic activity. It involves taking experience, exploring it, setting it into new contexts and examining what the outcome is in the short term and what may become of it in the longer view. Every interpretation, therefore, whether spoken or written, is temporary and in one sense naturally ephemeral. Yet at the same time, if they are accurately addressed, interpretations should also convey a sense of completeness: they pull together into new coherence aspects of life and experience which had hitherto appeared disparate.

When, however, we examine the contemporary style of interpretations in the media, we can discern a subtle change. No one doubts the ephemeral nature of interpretations offered on radio and television or in the press. The short life-span of a programme or a comment, even if at the time it seems weighty and enduring, is an obvious fact of media life. But it also seems to give the idea of 'completeness' a different sense. Instead of drawing disparate factors together and inviting further reflection on them, which leads to action or change, this type of interpretation implies a rounded conclusion.

An example of this may be drawn from the Project. At one point the participants became aware of this process in the reporting of events from South Africa, which at the time dominated the news. An episode would be presented and the reporter, as best as he or she could, would set it in some sort of context for the potential viewer in the United Kingdom. But they would frequently round off the piece with a concluding remark, as if the whole South African problem could somehow be contained and managed through this presentation. Viewers or listeners have their emotions energized, and probably feel anger, resentment or horror. Instead, however, of this part of their human experience being consciously and structurally related to other feelings and aspects of their life, and so made available for interpretation, it is locked away within the provided sense of totality.

Ministry, whether lay or ordained, consists of an interpretative stance. This will be affected by any prevailing expectation among people in general, and the ministers themselves, that any interpretation includes completion or rounding off. Indeed, this will be particularly true if the material to be interpreted is felt to be dangerous, threatening or disturbing. But since all experiences of life (especially those which the Church is invited to handle) are like this, the scope for exploratory interpretation in ministry will be implicitly restricted.

Similar difficulties may arise for any approach to education which involves exploring ideas by moving from hypothesis to hypothesis. This in practice underlies much theological training, but is in danger of seeming increasingly alien within the cultural context of the training programme as well as within the anticipated setting for future ministry. This is another field which is fundamentally affected by the existence of the media. It would appear to be a far more important factor for the whole issue of the communication of the gospel than some of the discussion of peripheral factors, such as the changing length of people's attention span and the like. Such technicalities matter, but not as much as the underlying expectation that is generated in people, which seems to govern what can be heard, received and responded to as opposed to noted, listened to and rounded off. Such 'packages' can than be set aside; an interpretative ministry and a learning programme that is consonant with it, however, are cumulative, requiring incompleteness in each hypothesis, so that all concerned can move onto the next.

THE ILLUSION OF INVULNERABILITY

In the media the illusion of invulnerability often appears to have to be sustained at any cost. This observation refers less to the difficulty that the media find in admitting error than to the way in which their existence creates a climate in which mistakes are feared. When the media err, they seem reluctant publicly to admit this. And because the media also possess instant access to archives (especially the powerful visual and aural ones), they also present an image of instant and unmerciful judgement. It is difficult, if not impossible, for anyone, once their views have been reported, to change their opinions, at least for public and rational reasons.

The impact of such invulnerability on individuals is becoming obvious. Public concern about this is being voiced at the time of writing (1989), with various proposals being made in Parliament about laws to protect privacy or compel restitution when publicity has been false or misleading. But educational and theological problems also occur. Error is an essential activity by which we learn. The nexus of experiment–error–correction–learning is enshrined in educational theory. If, however, error is perceived as a sign of weakness and recorded as something that may, and probably will, be reproduced in the future, caution against mistakes is likely to increase until educational endeavour as a whole declines. This is a concern over a much wider field than ours. But is also an issue here, especially since the process and style of interpretation in ministry is one of proceeding from hypothesis to hypothesis. In other words, there is a built-in vulnerability and positive commitment to risking error. This is fundamental to learning and to the practice of ministry, both of which cohere around the theme of vulnerability and invulnerability in a way which is essential if formation is to occur.

This connection between content and process around this theme is equally strong in theology. In the Christian scheme creative vulnerability is a primary model. The gospel proclaims that in Christ God makes himself uniquely vulnerable and because of this forgiveness is offered to men and women. This message is not falsified if the prevailing cultural assumption is one of defended invulnerability but it does become more difficult to frame and proclaim. In such a climate what meaning can be assigned to the idea of creative vulnerability and who can grasp it? The preacher may proclaim the words, but the hearers may be unable to comprehend the message.

FORGIVENESS AND RELATIONSHIPS

This is a further instance where the central issue is the cultural effect of the media not the specific content. An example may make this point clearer. In the previous chapter James Curran's comparison between the role of the Church in medieval society and that of the mass media in the contemporary world was discussed. A central issue was that of power and control. There are stimulating parallels to be drawn between the pervasive and permission-giving influence of today's mass media and that of the medieval Church. But a major difference between the two emerges when we consider forgiveness. That Church possessed power to bind in judgement but also, and more importantly, to loose: forgiveness was central to the life of the Church — how and by whom it could be offered and how it was to be earthed so that it could be experienced.

The media's capacity for offering forgiveness, if it exists at all, is limited. They are largely unforgiving. A person's past can be instantly recalled and used to confound them. The possibility of change and development is mentioned but in practice restricted. The same is true for a nation as a whole. It is not so much encouraged to learn from and build on its past as condemned continually to relive it. Theoretically the notion of putting events into context is excellent; but when it is actually attempted and the context consists of newsreel pictures or commentary, then it may become a constraint. Memory, instead of becoming selective and being integrated into one's sense of the past and so healed, is constantly re-awakened and the pains revived. If in a media-saturated world people experience life in this fashion, what sort of forgiveness can they look for, be offered and be capable of accepting?

If the context in which Christian interpretation (in this case of sin and forgiveness) is offered is one where the notion itself is suspect, then the form which that interpretation takes will need careful attention. The reactive tendency in today's Church is to say that the eternal gospel is not (and cannot be) changed because of altered circumstances. This response, however, overlooks the fact that this 'eternal gospel' itself has to take specific form. If, however, the language of a society — not just the words but its means of articulation — is changing subtly, but as significantly as these observations about the illusion of invulnerability might suggest, then the language of Christian interpretation will have to take this into account.

This century with its mass media is not the first occasion when such adjustment has been necessary. The original Gentile mission, the post-Constantinian period, and the Reformation were three such major steps in the history of Christian interpretation. The late twentieth century may be a time of similarly major transition, not only in social structures and the form of the Church, but also of the content of the gospel itself. Since, too, the context, because of the pervasiveness of the media, is now universal, the requirements of a 'universal' language for the interpretation of life through the gospel are more demanding. Simplistic application of 'Christian' language cannot constitute the ministerial and missionary task of interpretation.

We may illustrate this by briefly considering the connection between language and relationships. The style and content of religious language displays intimate links with personal relationships. Contemporary Christians are inclined to assert that the forms of communication which Christians employ can only be personal.

> Communication theorists as much as Christian moralists insist on a deep respect for the person communicated with. Christian communication must be interpersonal communication.[6]

This remark is unexceptionable, but may lead to a kind of idolatry of all that can be called 'personal'. The notion of relationship becomes affirmed almost for its own sake. It does not matter whether it be between an individual and God or between people. Its innate sanctity cannot be violated, least of all by any question of what it is for. In part this attitude may be a by-product of pastoral training, with the counselling emphases that prevail. It may also be connected with a spirituality which emphasizes personal formation. Whatever the reason, a sensitivity to questions of relationships is a mark of today's Church. They almost seem to be a modern sacred area.

This field of human relationships, however, may contribute to a supposed conflict between Churches and the media, especially television. Producers are accused of being intrusive or of trivializing what is profound, or, we might say, profaning that which is sacred. But in fact one of the major dangers inherent in presentations in the mass media is very similar to the religious idolizing of relationships. The relationship itself is portrayed as something desirable and to be achieved. Soap operas are an obvious instance.[7] Like the old morality plays, they present behaviour in relationships to which people may or may not aspire. Because, however, they are daily reiterations, they replace the notion that a relationship is created by the participants from what they contribute with a more mechanical idea of achieving an ideal state which has already been outlined.

The link between such an observation and theology is clear, with the two key themes of language and relationship coinciding. They are also significant in theological education. If, for instance, teaching about relationships on this assumption were to become the basis of pastoral practice, one result might be a tendency to oversimplify the idea of 'relationship'. In this way unwittingly a critical theological notion would begin to conform to one presented in the media as normal and often uncritically endorsed in caring stances.

Once again, therefore, fundamental questions of theology and issues raised by the existence of the modern media coincide. These topics are not just practical; they are seriously philosophical. Media issues, therefore, are not merely about how to do things.

TRUTH

Religion is concerned with truth, but never purely for its own sake. Religion is not philosophy. Religious truth is explored in the human contexts of what may be experienced and felt. The media are preoccupied with a similar issue. For example, it appears that in the media questions of truth are linked with those of sincerity. Direct connections seem to occur, for instance, between the apparent sincerity of a newscaster and the extent to which some people will believe the news to be true. The adage that you cannot lie to the camera because it will always expose you now looks like an apophthegm from earlier days when people were unfamiliar with the mass media and had less idea of how to use or abuse them. It has become a myth that may be repeated for reassurance but not for its accuracy.

Yet if falsehood is not self-evident in the media, neither is truth. Church leaders sometimes speak as if by contrast to such 'wordly' means of communication the Christian gospel carries intrinsic power because of its truth. There seems to be a wish to split essential gospel truth from evidently flawed presentations. But after McCluhan such a division is no longer sustainable, even if it ever was.

Divisions like this, however, still emerge in programmes of theological education. Questions of truth tend to be examined in sessions on philosophy and doctrine; those concerned with feelings are generally confined to pastoral studies and maybe liturgy. Yet it seemed to all participants in the Project, and from other discussions with ordinands and the newly ordained, that these two facets of learning comprise the crucial area of integration. This must be addressed, both for the sake of the practice of ministry and for exploring issues of the truth, and therefore the continuing adequacy, of the Christian gospel. Because the media are already in this field, it may be that some direct study of the way that they interrelate truth and feeling could be an indirect entry into the study of this area of contemporary human experience. Thence it could progress into powerful examination of, and learning about, integrated ministry.

CONCLUSION

Christian ministry is interpretative. Ministers are called to encounter people and, from whatever resource of the gospel they may have, they are expected to offer an interpretation of a fragment of human life. This may be powerfully individual, as in pastoral counsel. It may be more general, as in a sermon. But the stance is the same. In so acting, pastors also become theologians to themselves as well as to their congregations and, most importantly, to others.[8]

When we perceive this, connections between the media and ministry leap to mind. They do not seem far-fetched, but look inevitable. For, as we have noted, the media are today's primary conveyors of culture. They are both a creation and a creator of much of our contemporary life. They also provide the common forum in which people meet, especially where priest meets penitent, preacher meets congregation, and pastor meets those in need of counsel.

In this chapter we have noted how the task of interpretation is being affected by the prevalence of the modern mass media. On the whole it has been suggested that they are not malign but that their existence is changing the context of ministry more profoundly than the Churches' ministers have yet realized. Before we conclude, however, it is worth noting briefly a final observable effect of the media as a cultural phenomenon.

We are no longer naive enough to think that the media are 'controlled' only in totalitarian regimes. The present problems of regulation and deregulation alert us to the complexity of their place within a free society. But the more the mass media are used to present a particular vision, the more they seem to evoke dissent from it.

41

People might believe something because it was on the radio or TV or in the press, even though the connection is not as simple as was once thought. But there seem to be some other people who take a diametrically opposed stance: because something is in the media it is *not* to be believed. While, therefore, our world may be media-saturated, we should not assume that it is media-dominated. The media arouse dissent not because they are organs of opposition to prevailing power structures and the ethos of a society, but because, being so dominant, they stir the resisting parts at least in some people.

Interpretation is the key model of ministry. But behind this for the Christian faith, with its emphasis upon the word and proclamation, there remains a necessary discomfort: What is it to *communicate* the gospel, even if we see such communication in the context of interpretation? A second question arises in the light of our discussion of the media, particularly as a cultural phenomenon: Is there a distinctive way in which the media as phenomenon contribute to the educational theory required for contemporary theological education? The first of these two questions is addressed in the final chapter of this section. The second forms the foundation for Part II.

Notes

1. John Corner and Jeremy Hawthorn, eds, *Communication Studies* (London, Edward Arnold, 2nd edn 1985), p. 145.

2. Denis McQuail, 'The influence and effects of mass media', in James Curran, Michael Gurevitch and Janet Woollacott, eds, *Mass Communication and Society* (London, Edward Arnold, 1977), p. 87.

3. Stewart M. Hoover, *Mass Media Religion: The Social Sources of the Electronic Church* (Newbury Park, California, Sage, 1988).

4. '"Interpretation" does not correspond exactly to the German word "*Deutung*". The English term tends to bring to mind the subjective—perhaps even the forced or arbitrary—aspects of the attribution of a meaning to an event or statement. "*Deutung*" would seem to be closed to "explanation" or "clarification" and, in common usage, has fewer of the pejorative overtones that are at times carried by the English word. Freud writes that the *Deutung* of a dream consists in ascertaining its *Bedeutung* or meaning.' J. Laplanche and J-B.

Pontalis, *The Language of Psychoanalysis* (London, Hogarth Press, 1973), p. 228.

5. Wesley Carr, *The Priestlike Task* (London, SPCK, 1985); *The Pastor as Theologian* (London, SPCK, 1989).

6. R. T. Brooks, *Communicating Conviction* (London, Epworth, 1983), p. 109.

7. John Lippman, 'Pulling the Plug on the Soaps', *Sunday Times* 21 May 1989, suggests that the era of soap operas is over. Even if this is the case, it seems likely that some such repetitive dramas will remain an ingredient of television. It looks as though the implausibility of some of the American productions has lost them their audience.

8. Carr, *The Pastor as Theologian.*

3 COMMUNICATING RELIGIOUS IDEAS

'Communication' is a reassuring notion; 'media' is too vast, complex, value laden and possibly not a suitable topic for those whose task is to think theologically. 'Communication', by contrast, sounds a legitimate topic for investigation and study, not least since the communication of the gospel has always been a priority for the Church. Thinking about communication allows us to split reflection and practice. Communications studies can be explored philosophically, with attention given to psychology and sociology. The practice of communicating can be regarded as a matter of acquiring a skill.

But communications studies, without the controlling referent of the modern media, can (and in practice also seem to) drift into culturally non-specific learning. For example, a course may begin with study of God's communication and slide into an aspect of doctrinal studies of Jesus and the incarnation or of the idea of revelation. The course thus retreats from the harsh demands of the media environment — how do we communicate the notion of 'God'? — to the more familiar, and therefore more comfortable, internal concerns of the Christian tradition.

PASTORING AND COMMUNICATION

The word 'communication' has become prominent in church debates. Communications' Officers have been appointed. Their responsibilities are usually ill-defined, ranging widely from improving in-house communications to enabling ministers and congregations to evangelize more effectively. Whenever their work is questioned it is justified by such slogans as 'Communication is the essence of the gospel', or 'Without communication there can be no truly human life'. But while such resonant claims are impressive, the experience of the role is frequently one of uncertainty about its limits. The officers are unclear what they are precisely to do; church people are unwilling to recognize that the officer has any specific authority; and those outside the Church find his comments incomprehensible.

This half caricature of communications' officers brings the term 'communication' alive. We have already registered the problems around the word 'media'; similar difficulties arise with 'communication'. Indeed, we might say that to define 'communication' would be to remove the richness of the concept and so diminish rather than clarify the field of study. For instance, if we are too precise, how will we acknowledge the connection between verbal and non-verbal forms of communication?

Communication, conveying a message, is an essential skill of pastors. They both speak the gospel and are expected by others to embody it. Such ministry demands more than the occasional course of preaching. We are addressing a vast dimension of contemporary life, which is particularly significant in our culture. In order, therefore, to root such a wide-ranging topic, it seems sensible to be concerned with communication in the specific setting of the media.

It is sometimes suggested that the Churches' concern should be with communication rather than with the media. There is a superficial attraction in the suggestion. For instance, communication theory includes study of signs and symbols, as well as human rituals. These are the day-to-day concerns of the priest or minister. Or again, communication is a live issue both in the congregational setting and in pastoral engagement with others. Edmund Leach's comment demonstrates this, especially if we substitute 'congregation' for 'company of close friends' and 'other pastoral contacts' for 'strangers':

> When we are in the company of close friends [congregation] and neighbours we all take it for granted that communication is a complex continuous process which has many non-verbal as well as verbal components. It is only when we meet with strangers [other pastoral contacts] that we suddenly become aware that, because all customary behaviour (and not just acts of speech) convey information, we cannot understand what is going on until we know the code.[1]

COMMUNICATING RELIGIOUS EXPERIENCE

For Christians one of the most familiar forms of attempted communication is the sermon. The preacher is a key person, especially in the Protestant tradition, although increasingly, too, in the Roman Catholic Church. One preacher reported the following comment made to him during a visit:

> 'I don't always *understand* what he [the preacher] says, but I *feel* it is important. Sometimes he really speaks to me; sometimes I feel it ought to mean more. But he always makes me *think* and I know that my life is *changing*.'

This remark is reported *verbatim* from a person who regularly attends church. It is especially interesting because it contains the basic ingredients which we have to take into account when thinking about the communication of religious ideas. The four words in italics, when put together, encompass the complex of notions with which we are dealing: understanding, feeling, thought and change. Any one of these cannot be separated from another without denying an aspect of religious experience.

Religious experience is not confined by doctrine or tradition. But no one is immune from their cultural and inherited backgrounds and hence no one is completely isolated from a particular form of religious expression. This may be general — e.g. Christian, Jewish, Hindu, Muslim; or it may also be more specific — e.g. Anglican, Roman Catholic, Methodist, Baptist. Religious experience cannot occur without implicit shaping from a particular tradition. This does not mean that a person remains locked within that tradition or even that he or she, while standing within it, accepts it all. But 'understanding', a way of speaking and thinking which has been articulated by others and with which we can associate (or from which we can dissociate), is an ingredient in religious experience.

While at some times and in certain Christian traditions people have been wary about the place of feelings, today they are acknowledged as a key facet of religious experience. When we say this, however, we may be referring to two areas, both of which are important.

By 'feelings' we may mean states of feeling, such as sadness or joy, ecstasy or despair. Mainstream religions and their leaders customarily mistrust and warn against these, while those nearer the fringe indulge them. They are the uncontrolled, and therefore to a degree uncontrollable, dimension of religious activity and are often associated with dissent and fundamentalism. Such feelings are, however, a necessary aspect of the complex of religious experience and cannot be disregarded.

Today, however, 'feelings' refer also to the dimension of the unconscious mind and the way in which its processes interact with our conscious selves. The boundary, for instance, between religious belief and the irrational can now not only be explored but acknowledged as significant. Religion and irrationality are intimately connected, but in most reflection on religion and belief, the second dimension is not usually given attention. This avoidance may itself be a contributory factor to the problems of religious communication, not least since psychologically oriented approaches are so prominent in other areas of contemporary life.

Third in the list we have 'thinking'. Superficially this may seem to be an alternative for 'understanding'. But in this discussion 'understanding' represents the framework of assumptions which are the first reference for feeling. 'Thinking' by contrast occurs as we relate feeling to that framework. This is a reflective activity through which in practice faith is generated. This process has usually, but not always, been acknowledged by religious teachers. Feelings alone are insufficient to lead to genuine faith; they are too subjective to be saving, since they tend to become locked within the self and hinder development. Tradition or learning, too, suffers from a similar weakness. It is, as it were, too objective to be saving, since it remains outside the self. Faith comes about as heart (here-and-now emotion and feeling) and head (learned understanding) interact through the reflective process of thinking.

The last word in this sequence refers to the product of religious activity—change. Although religious people themselves offer various tests of their beliefs—truth, conformity to tradition, intensity of experience and the like—the ultimate test of religious belief is its effect, the degree to which people's lives, those of the adherents and those of others, are significantly affected. Change, salvation, and activity with God take precedence over preoccupation with feeling or learning. Rabbi Bunam, according to an old Hasidic story, honoured a man in his House of Prayer by asking him to blow the ram's horn at the festival. As the man began to make lengthy preparations to concentrate on the meaning of the sounds, the rabbi cried out: 'Fool, go ahead and blow!' 'By their fruits you shall know them.'

This outline, sketchy as it is, demonstrates the problems in communicating religious ideas. For each of these four facets is directed to different responding parts of the person: the cultural, inherited self, with whom we struggle throughout our lives, although most notably during adolescence; the unconscious mind of which, by its nature, we are rarely aware; the reflective self, which is so overworked by living that it is difficult to particularize it to one area of life, such as, for example, the religious; and the changing or developing self, which is inevitably unsure of itself.

We are, therefore, dealing with a dimension of human life which is larger and more complex than most professionally religious people realize. The subject is correspondingly imprecise. Religious awareness, which gives rise to religious ideas, only exists because human beings have been, and still are, troubled and at times excited by questions to which no satisfactory answer can be given. Religious awareness is continuously being negotiated between social and cultural elements and individual insights and demands from the experience of living. From time to time, as perhaps is happening at present, the sense becomes stronger that the old languages, symbols and rituals are failing to connect with the questions which still disturb people. But that is always likely to be arguable and in such times it is a mistake to confuse dissatisfaction with formal means of religious expression with a collapse of religion.[2]

COMMUNICATION AND THE THREE MOODS OF RELIGIOUS LANGUAGE

Given these difficulties, care is needed lest believers try to hide their frustrations with the current place of religious institutions in people's lives, including their own, behind the contemporary and approved concept of 'communication'. 'Religious ideas' is an imprecise notion; the associated concept of 'communication' also resists clarity. We need, therefore, not so much a perfect structure for thinking about these questions as some signposts in a confused and confusing field.

Religious language oscillates between statement (which tends to be found in ritual formularies), tentative inarticulateness and longing language. The moods of the verbs in such discourse are, therefore, indicative, subjunctive and optative. All three moods are together present somewhere in a religious remark.

(a) Indicative

In the use of indicative language lie many of the Church's contemporary difficulties in providing the framework for understanding which people can use as they explore religious issues. The Christian liturgies, for instance, with their emphasis on Scripture being read in an undifferentiated fashion and the implicit literalism which results, appear to close down options rather than increase them. There is a difference between offering the opportunity of the process of worship and demanding total involvement (and by implication agreement) with all that is said and done.

The tradition of proclamation may saddle the Christian Church with a restricted view of communication as a movement from 'us' to 'them': the Church has the gospel; people have to hear it. This assumption is rejected by the process of communication in our more interactive world. Indicative language is today heard not so much as proclaiming a truth which requires assent (agreement) as offering and maintaining usable markers which invite involvement (interpretation). When we perceive this, our concept of the Church's functioning is changed. As a repository of the tradition, it should prove itself reliable. The Church will, therefore, inevitably tend to be conservative in its rituals and activity but not in its members' use of the tradition in interpreting life with their neighbours.

(b) Subjunctive

Subjunctive language expresses the questioning and exploring aspect of religious awareness. In this, too, a new factor is today involved: we are invited to move in two directions at once. Neither is new, but their congruence seems to represent a new phase in mankind's history.

On the one hand we are probing deeper into the self. We are more self-aware than our predecessors and, as a result, less certain of who we are. The psychology of the individual and the behaviour of groups are so exposed to scrutiny that we become tentative. Those who have the intellectual and emotional strength to live with this are wary of commitment; others instinctively deny this side of their nature and irrationally assert themselves.

On the other hand, we are simultaneously bombarded with images and explorations which take us beyond ourselves, or at least beyond worlds with which we can cope. Television in particular disturbs our familiar, local universe, so that we decreasingly know for what we can be held responsible, what belongs to us and what does not.

Such conditions, however, are precisely those where religious awareness should become more acute but where any specific tradition or particular religion will seem decreasingly relevant in its affirmations. D. W. Winnicott in exploring the psychological development of people noted that illusion is essential to the child's development and that it continues in significance throughout adult life:

> I am studying the substance of *illusion,* that which is allowed to the infant, and which in adult life is inherent in art and religion, and yet becomes the hallmark of madness when an adult puts too powerful a claim on the credulity of others, forcing them to acknowledge a sharing of illusion that is not their own.[3]

Illusion is formed in the negotiation that takes place between our inner and outer worlds. It does not describe the whole of this very complicated interaction, but it draws attention to the way in which we are both created by and create our own worlds.

In this brief outline we may discern an important link which is useful when considering the communication of religious ideas. Art is inextricably caught up in a society, and especially the importance it assigns to leisure. In our societies leisure, as we have already noted, is plentiful and will become more so. But our new space is being filled by the products of the communications industries, the media.

It is sometimes glibly said that television is good at places and people, but not at handling abstract concepts, such as religious ideas. This, however, is too simple; television is more than merely a communications' vehicle. It is becoming, if it is not already, a major art form. Here the tendency for religious people to become concerned with the content of programmes and to overlook the significance of the process of their communication is especially dangerous. People today live with highly stimulated imaginations; we are bombarded with images, visual and aural.

The task of religious believers then becomes not one of trying to impose their patterns upon these images but of offering opportunities for interpreting them. The communication of religious ideas, therefore, is akin to art criticism.

Peter Armstrong, a well-known maker of religious television programmes, including *Sea of Faith,* writes:

> Christian truths must always be clothed in the particular metaphorical language that is appropriate to the contemporary culture. The task is not to demythologize, but to remythologize. This may seem hopelessly haphazard to the theologians who try to systematize religious language; . . . in that I believe that religious myths and metaphors must, if they are to be of any interest, refer to a transcendent rather than to a subjective reality, there is no possible process by which they can be checked against it.[4]

As an expert in the field, Armstrong instinctively grasps that communication is not directed but negotiated. A programme of remythologizing is not one of return to old images and rituals in the hope that they may recover their power. It rather requires us to relate new images to the tradition in such a way that the experience which demands that we make the attempt is not destroyed in a misconceived battle over what is true. Two aspects to this are particularly important.

First, there is one that has already been mentioned: the Church's inevitable conservatism in sustaining the origins of its traditions as reference points by which others can order their new images and experiences. As Armstrong again puts it:

> For me, today's icon of innocent suffering can only be the painfully familiar newspaper image of the starving child, and I would start there in the exploration of what the sacrifice of Christ might mean to the late twentieth century.[5]

But without people who believe in the specific significance of the sacrifice of Christ, the image becomes so generalized as to be ineffectual. The widespread use of religious, specifically Christian, imagery may depend more than we realize upon its being sustained in its particular religious context. Here the indicative language of tradition and the subjunctive words of contemporary images coincide.

Second, there is always a risk that questions of truth may be lost in the struggle to interpret and reinterpret. Sometimes church authorities have tried to impose checks on the range of human experience. 'Orthodoxy' thus becomes the presumed test of what people are allowed to feel. But since there can be no control in this area of people's lives, the inevitable outcome is that they disregard the imposition. Truth questions in religion are those which consistently push all, whatever their precise belief or state of feeling, into that area of fundamental exploring which was, and which remains, the origin and sustaining force for religion and without which there can be no religious experience. Theology, therefore, as a critical and intellectual discipline retains its significance.

(c) Optative

There is a third dimension to religious language and ideas. The optative mood expresses longing or wish: 'O that this were so!' Such longing brings us to the core of religious experience. Rarely do we merely affirm that something is the case; more often we express a cry of longing on behalf of ourselves and others. This cry, or prayer, lies at the heart, for example, of the profoundest religious experience of God. The intense longing for the vision of God is matched only by the longing to be free of the constraints which such a vision brings. As Newman saw in *The Dream of Gerontius,* the result of the soul's longing to be with God can only be the anguished cry, 'Take me away!', when the majesty of God is dimly perceived. While such optative language may be immature and simplistic, it also directs attention to a key facet of what goes under the heading of religious experience and may paradoxically discourage complacency, especially in the sophisticated and professionally religious. For ministers the practicalities of the optative (the human dimension not of belief or knowledge, but of longing) are an essential ingredient of their pastoral activity.

CONCLUSION

Communication is a negotiated activity. It is not, therefore, a matter of being concerned about getting a message over. Religious ideas and the concept of communication both indicate that we are in a world which we create rather than one which we inhabit. Religious ideas operate in the interstices of our human make-up. They are, therefore, inevitably felt to be dangerous.

Those who believe that they understand these things tend towards control (orthodoxy); those who have little or nothing to do with them try to diminish their importance (apathy). No appreciation of communication will assist us in this persistent dilemma, but equally attention to the media and communication may direct theological studies to the central area of Christian anthropology and pastoral understanding.

Since imagination is a key to religious awareness, the communication of religious ideas is likely to be tangential rather than direct. For instance, it may be a wise strategy of a Church which wishes to share its awareness of God, to engage less in evangelism (whether discussion about it or attempts at it) and more in trying to ensure that people's imagination and their ability to articulate thoughts in connection with it are sustained.

Notes

1. Edmund Leach, *Culture and Communication: The Logic by which Symbols are Connected* (Cambridge, CUP, 1976), p. 9.

2. David Hay, *Exploring Inner Space* (Harmondsworth, Penguin Books, 1982), p. 212.

3. D. W. Winnicott, 'Transitional objects and transitional phenomena', in *The Maturational Process and the Facilitating Environment* (London, Hogarth Press, 1965), p. 230.

4. Peter Armstrong, 'Television as a Medium for Theology', in Peter Eaton, ed., *The Trial of Faith* (Worthing, Churchman Publishing, 1988), p. 192.

5. ibid.

Part Two

INTRODUCTION

In the next four chapters we shall address some of the major issues which emerge from consistently thinking about the Church and theology in the light of the media.

First, we shall examine how the media set the context within which the Church today offers its ministry. This is an extension of some of the ideas offered in Part I. But they are now placed explicitly alongside questions about the nature of the Church and its theological endeavours.

Second, we shall consider some of the profound and persistent issues which religion addresses and the way that in the modern world the media contribute to their identification and definition.

Third, we shall propose the media as a holding context—that is, a means of sustaining coherence and order—for any programme which takes theological reflection as its focus. This phrase 'theological reflection' is today widely used in exploration into the nature of the Church's life. For example, it is proposed as a skill to be inculcated in ordinands; in a more general sense it describes what should be the instinctive stance of any Christian. Like any jargon, however, it needs to be clarified. We can achieve this if we move out of the restricted environment of the Church and think in terms of the wider culture, as represented by the media. 'Interpretation', which was discussed in Chapter 2, is now specifically applied to the theme of theological reflection.

Each chapter is complete in itself, but the theoretical argument runs through all of them. Any point, then, which in the first or second chapters seems unduly obscure, should become clearer when all four have been read and an overview of the issues has been acquired.

4 THE MEDIA AS CONTEXT

How do we discern the context in which the Church's ministry is exercised? Even more difficult, how do we begin to think about the future setting and prepare for life in the next generation? In preparing ministers and training Christians today much attention has rightly been paid to the content and process of programmes. Less, however, has been directed to examining the various contexts of the Church and its ministry. Most of these are derived from sociological studies or pastors' anecdotes. But the moment we regard the media as a significant factor in contemporary life, they make the question of context paramount.

A MEDIA-SATURATED ENVIRONMENT

However we describe the environment in which the Churches now work, one point is indisputable: we live in a media-saturated environment. 'Saturated' is a better term than the more frequently employed 'dominated', since the latter implies an unexamined stance of judgement on the media. Our culture is not saturated simply in terms of the amount of material available on radio, television and in the press. Nor are the reported statistics of those who view, read or listen the key factor. We are speaking of the total culture to which the media contribute and with which they interact. Even though the major media vary in their impact on people, this does not mean that we cannot describe our society as 'media-saturated'. It is more easy to avoid reading a newspaper than to turn off the television. Television is notably more intrusive than radio—at least to those brought up before its widespread availability. But in spite of such qualifications, 'media-saturated' describes the society which we know and of which we are members. Wherever we turn there is no avoiding the direct or dispersed impact of the mass media.

As we have noted, the term 'media', while problematic, is

useful so long as it is not defined too precisely. Its plural form indicates that it refers to a range of material and means, as well as concepts and values. The phrase 'mass media' in particular carries overtones of power; it is rarely used in a good sense. It seems to suggest disapproval, as if we would be better off without them but we have unfortunately to put up with them. And the word 'media' in its strict sense, that is, that which mediates or moves between, includes both producer, purveyor and consumer. In other words, 'media' is a concept which becomes all-embracing in its use, regardless of any precise evidence about the impact of the media on people's lives.

Yet these are also exactly aspects of our contemporary societies which cause general disarray. They are not peculiar to the media. For instance, a pluralist environment is welcomed because it is rich and comprehensive. But for many it simultaneously generates uncertainty, and often regret, because boundaries become unclear. Where, for example, do the inherited ethnic and religious aspects of life coincide with or conflict with the overarching requirements of one nation? It is perhaps not surprising in the light of such a question to discover that the United States, with its high-profile religious and ethnic groups, but also its strong sense of being American, is the place where the mass media have become most prominent and where they have originated many of their own norms.

Again, we might reflect on the issue of where power lies and how it is to be employed in a democracy. This question fascinates but worries. What constitutes such power? Who possesses it? What is its legitimation? This fundamental problem is especially acute in a democracy but even more so when that democratic order exists in a plural setting. Yet this massive question is focused with distinctive clarity in the fact of the media.

The linking of purveyor and consumer, which we have noted in the media, is another general issue in a complex society. The recent (1989) confusion in Great Britain over responsibility for food production—the so-called 'salmonella scare'—is a good example. Was this to fall to the Ministry of Agriculture, which is identified in the public mind with the purveyor, or to the Ministry of Health, which notionally is concerned for the consumer? Where do producers and consumers stand in relation to one another, especially in terms of their respective rights and duties? Again the problem does not belong to the mass media: it is endemic in contemporary society. But it becomes specifically explorable and addressable in consideration of the media.

While, therefore, it may be a fruitless exercise to try and define the term 'media', it by no means follows that the concept becomes unusable. On the contrary, it looks potentially like a useful means through which to grapple with many of the large issues of the world in which the Church exercises its ministry and proclaims the gospel. And in today's complexities the concept of 'media', especially 'mass media', may provide what we may call 'locatable imprecision'. In other words, by focusing upon the range of associations with the term, we can make sufficiently specific, and hence locatable, many of the issues facing Churches and ministers, without so defining them that we lose contact with the actual confusion of living.

MEDIA AS A CULTURAL PHENOMENON

If, however, we were to select one perspective on the media as especially significant, it would be their existence as a cultural phenomenon. Every society possesses culturally accepted places, where its members expect to find certain subject matters. This may be, for instance, the lore which was possessed in earlier times by priests or lawgivers. It could be said of such societies that 'everyone knows' that information about how to live will be obtained from them. In a more stratified society, the different roles of individuals or groups within it are to some extent defined by the knowledge that they possess and the accessibility that they allow others to have to it. In our present world, much (indeed almost all) of our information, whether about ourselves or our world, is mediated through modern means of communication.

But there are more of these than the mass media alone. For example, our sense of the self in relation to others is altered when telephones or new means of transport change the distance involved in that relationship. The shape of the world itself, if drawn in terms of accessibility rather than by geography, is very different from the maps with which most are familiar. London and New York are, thanks to Concorde, about the same distance apart as, say, London and Manchester. Satellite links bring countries into different proximity. In Bristol I can probably know more quickly about what may be happening in Afghanistan than I do about what is happening a street away. And it is a commonplace joke, but also a parable, that a transglobal telephone call will be clearer and quicker than one to a near neighbour.

This revolution in communications forces us to adjust our perception of who we are and the contexts in which we live. In most cases this change is not traumatic; we just get on with life. But the underlying effect may be more significant. Since much information is transmitted through the new means of communication, we can with reason speak of ours as a 'communications culture'. This affects our social institutions because of the different degree of association with them that is now possible. It was strange, in an earlier chapter, to recall Churchill's fears in 1953 lest the mystery of royalty were to be profaned. But the arguments offered against televising Parliament in 1989 are not so dissimilar.

Social institutions, however, are not only affected by new forms of communication. They are also being created anew by interaction with them. When someone produces a reflective study on the effect of the mass media on the idea of royalty, this will probably become instantly clear. In Great Britain the royal family offers a fascinating instance of creative interaction with the media. In the United States a similar process can be discerned in the way that the President is made and sustained. Those who know, or learn, how to interact with (which is different from attempting to manipulate) the media, such as the Queen or President Reagan, are as much created as any. Perhaps their secret is the extent to which they know it.

Within this communications' age, the mass media hold a distinctive place in relation to culture and social structure. But here, too, the idea of interaction remains dominant. A social structure is constantly being constructed and reconstructed. It is neither given, requiring the media to present it, nor created by the media and so offered to people. In other words, the media are not, as is sometimes assumed, 'out there' influencing us, whether individuals or society. They are a major means in today's world by which the concepts of ourselves, of others and of society, with which we each work, are constantly generated.

FOUR ISSUES FOR CONSIDERATION

Recognizing this, and acknowledging that when we speak of 'media' we are talking about something ultimately indefinable but sensed and discernible, we discover that four major issues emerge. Each is indicated by the existence and activity of the media. But each also lies as a topic at the heart of contemporary Christian life and witness.

(a) The Managerial Issue

In a complex society, a basic experience for many seems to be that of being lost in places which are expected to be familiar.[1] We are probably more acutely aware of ourselves than any previous generation. We have learned that as persons we are not quite what we thought we were. But few, if any, feel clearer as to what or who they exactly are. For example, the argument over the relative importance for the individual of heredity or environment implies this question. This experience might be more bearable were there some other fixed points by which to orient ourselves in our world.

But our institutions are also changing. The markers by which people used to map their progression through life seem to be moved. We lack any obvious foci in which to place confidence that we can know who we are and where we fit in. These are not despairing observations, for the experience is not of the world as a whole crumbling around us. The customary markers of relationships, family life, commerce and social intercourse remain, even if in some respects changed. But these 'familiar places' do not function in the way that they once seemed to in order to provide us with a sense of our place in the world.

The media are sometimes accused of having brought about this state of affairs. They promulgate, so it is claimed, a view of the world which is destructive rather than creative and deceptive rather than honest. The suggestion has been made with vigour by, for example, Malcolm Muggeridge.[2] There may be some truth in it. But the modern media are as much products of the context as its cause.

This contention can be illustrated by an example drawn from the major previous change in mass media—the invention of printing in 1476. That technological breakthrough had profound social consequences. But it also came about because at that moment the developing societies of Europe and the expanding range of knowledge demanded something of the sort. Today's mass media seem to be a similar case. They are extraordinary technological achievements, which have become possible because something like them is needed. The complexity of social interactions in the world at large, and those microcosms of it which are represented by pluralist societies, require means by which some sort of culture can be sustained and transmitted.

A pluralist society presents us with endless complications of values, beliefs and rituals. There is, therefore, an endemic question in life as to how to cope with these. This is the managerial question. How do I manage myself and those with me in such a way as to survive and, if possible, contribute something to the world? This is the theme of many dramas. The news on radio and television, too, is largely presented in terms of this question. Most human interest stories fall within its range. We are delighted to see good 'managers', those who cope; we are saddened when 'management', both social and individual, collapses; and we sympathize out of our own predicament with those who, like most of us, struggle in the middle.

These issues are profoundly religious and specifically significant for the Christian Churches. How are they and Christian individuals to cope with the complexities of the world in which they find themselves? The problem may be posed as if it were outside the Church: 'Why do more people not believe the gospel?' Or it may be regarded as a question of Christian living: 'How are we to continue to believe in the face of modern ways of thinking?' But the ultimate effect is the same: we feel lost in the very places which are supposed to feel familiar and reassuring.

It is to this experience that Christian ministers are asked to address themselves. It emerges in demands for clearer teaching. Fundamentalist stances, whether biblical, traditional or charismatic, are one response. Even that which is characterized as a relativistic response sometimes looks uncannily similar, a fundamentalism of relativism.

A parallel demand may appear for more competent leadership on the part of the minister. He or she is then required to become a surrogate boundary marker, by which others can orient themselves. Personal charisma begins to seem an essential attribute of ministry. The implicit ideals of management that this demand represents need to be understood by ministers, if they are not to find themselves trapped in illusions about the nature of their ministry.

These issues are not being created by the media. But the media, as a function of the modern world, provide a locus in which they can be exposed and explored, so that learning can come about. For the issue of self-management, so central to contemporary living, is also an essential question for ministers.

(b) The Evidential Problem

However they are understood in the modern world, modern communications, and the mass media in particular, are a major force. According to some—for example, those espousing the Muggeridgean position—they are a malign influence. But this is too simplistic. The media are so pervasive that people are caught between what they feel, as their lives seem affected, and what they can test.

Anxious attention is paid to the effects that the media may have upon people. There are occasional notorious instances when someone seems to, and may even claim to, act under the direct influence of what he or she has seen on television or film. Massacres, such as that at Hungerford in 1987 or the Californian school in 1989, are linked with the portrayal of violence on the screen. Sexual crime is associated with pornographic material. These are the highly publicized instances. But since people can feel in themselves the way that their emotions are stirred by dramatic pictures, there is a sort of personal *a priori* which says that the media must be having such an influence. Plato said that dramatic portrayal of people in emotional states should be banned from the perfect republic, since they 'water that which is best kept dry'.[3]

Yet once the emotional flush of assumptions has run its course and is replaced with a more reflective stance and cool rationality, a familiar consequence ensues. It proves impossible to demonstrate any direct connection between individual behaviour and what has been viewed that all agree.

A series of studies in the United States, beginning with Congressional hearings as early as 1950, has shown links between visual images and individual and social behaviour. Various commissions have been significant enough to disturb the main producers of material for television. But the most careful research includes this as one of its outcomes:

> Although it is *technically impossible* to prove a cause-and-effect relationship in most field studies, the vast majority of such studies demonstrates a positive association between exposure to media violence and agressiveness.[4]

This is not the place to rehearse the debate. The fact that it occurs, however, highlights another aspect of the world in which the Churches have to exercise their ministry. We find it hard to get our feeling self and our thinking self in harmony. In the case of violence, for instance, we instinctively feel that it is having an effect on us and hence on others. But when we are made to examine the topic rationally, we cannot exactly match that feeling with our thinking. In other words, it is difficult enough to discover the extent to which the media have direct influence on people; it is even harder to discover what would constitute evidence for such believed influence.

The issue here is more acute than the age-old debate over the question of aesthetic judgement in matters of art and religion. The media intertwine content and process in such a way that coherent discussion has become unusually problematic for sophisticated people. Those, therefore, who are regarded as opinion formers compete with differing opinions, the merits of which are difficult to weigh, since what might constitute evidence has become too problematic to discern, agree and discuss. Among such opinion formers and teachers are the Churches' ministers. They find themselves struggling in this role. They share the general uncertainty about how to evaluate the extent of the media's influence on belief and behaviour.

But they also find that the same questions arise in their own field of theology and pastoral practice. Again, therefore, we observe that a key issue for ministry in general may be focused through thinking about the media. Religious belief in God, for example, increasingly suffers from incoherence. On the one hand, there remains ample evidence that religious feelings are still felt, even in a secular society. Religious experience is not the prerogative of professed believers. David Hay is one who has experimentally tested this.[5] Others have examined the continuing dimension of transcendence.[6] Cumulatively such studies demonstrate that immanence and transcendence remain matters of believed experience rather than theoretical doctrines alone. On the other hand, the Churches, the recognized bodies for handling such feelings, seem to be losing their ability to help people locate such heart feelings with the head framework that they need.

There is, therefore, in the field of belief a new dimension to the question of what would constitute evidence. Feelings have their place, but are by themselves insufficient. Data, by contrast, seem infinitely collectable but almost impossible to relate with confidence either to feelings or to any framework of thought. The evidential question, therefore, which is acutely raised by the media, also lies at the heart of the Churches' efforts to offer the Christian gospel. Once again we discover that we are taken tangentially through attention to a primary facet of contemporary culture—the media—into a familiar area of critical study about the nature of faith and some of the concerns to do with its proclamation. Such learning is essential for any who wish to minister in today's world.

(c) The Moral Issue

High on the list of topics which the media disturb is morality. The values displayed by characters in dramas, and especially soap operas, are criticized. Indeed, in the popular press, which is linked to television in a sort of media narcissism, confusion between the morals of the characters and those of the actors and actresses who play them is a staple diet. Concern with the cardinal sins remains a legitimate Christian occupation. But the mass media require modern Churches and their ministers to face the more serious moral dimensions to modern life than those of personal behaviour.

Power is a major topic: Who possesses it and how should it be sanctioned? The new communications have changed the arena in which debate takes place. As public service broadcasting gives way to a commercial approach, problems about whose voice the audience is hearing will become more acute. This question is not solely about commercial control. After all, in the early days of broadcasting, it is arguable that the voice being chiefly heard was that of Sir John Reith.[7] But as the mass media become increasingly universal in their scope, concern begins to emerge about who owns these powerful means of communication.

Perhaps this will become more serious as with the greater number of channels the amount of discussion will increase. Talking-heads are cheap, but nonetheless effective. In a world with so many voices, the dilemma becomes first, Who is behind them and with what motives? and second, Is every voice of equal value?

Another area of the media where morality is a concern is advertising. This existed long before the modern media but these have extended its potential influence. Advertisers and the consumer ethic which drives them, have been heavily criticized from various sources, including the Churches. Although the effectiveness of advertising on purchasing is disputed, the number of publications of technical journals suggests that those most involved have some anxiety. This may be whether such advertising is a form of brainwashing (Vance Packard) and whether it encourages the inequality of distribution of the world's resources (John Kenneth Galbraith).[8] There are also issues to do with the economic interdependence of advertisers and commercial programme makers, including what Postman called 'the flight from reason'.

This set of issues coalesces in the fact of the media, which once again directs our attention to underlying issues in the society of which the Churches are part. Fulmination has little effect. Simplistic moral stances are self-defeating and therefore excluded in a media-saturated society.

Interestingly, the moral dimension to life, which the mass media are exposing in new ways, is likely to return to theological investigation those moral and political questions which have recently declined in prominence. We might speculate, for instance, that the way in which in Great Britain the Churches and the government seem to be in conflict over the nature of society is one example of a change in the ground rules for moral debate. Moral and political thinking are being drawn more closely together, as a result of people beginning to perceive that the central moral problem of this age concerns the exercise of power and authority.

To these and similar topics the existence of the media undoubtedly makes a contribution. For our purposes, however, we may again note how a dimension of contemporary life which is highlighted by media questions — the moral dimension — is also crucial in ministry. Pastors report that moral guidance is increasingly demanded of them and that they feel less competent to give it than they would wish. Church leaders have a similar experience with the demand for comment and leadership. Yet much moral teaching in courses of theological education seems to have been unable to base itself in this reality. It seems either to deal with small 'sins' or with global issues. The grey areas in which people actually live are overlooked. A participant in the Project expressed this succinctly:

> Some ethical values as portrayed in the media are contrary to Christian ethical standards. I don't really find this threatening — just a fact of reality. But at times I might feel that the world is saying to those in training, 'Come on, this *is* the twentieth century.'

(d) The Extensial Issue

The fourth issue relates to the previous three, but can be separately identified: Is there a definable limit to the extent of the media's influence, actual or potential? There is no adjective that adequately describes this dimension, so for convenience I coin the neologism *extensial*.

A genuine hermit might claim to live beyond the influence of the media and so represent a limit. Indeed, a modern definition of a hermit might be 'someone without a television set'. But that would be a false assumption. Hermits are products of the society which they are rejecting. They represent one facet of that society, which others are unable or unwilling to sustain. People, therefore, who believe (or of whom others believe) that because they have no television they live beyond the influence of the media are mistaken.

> The major function of advertising is to open the way for marketing by creating styles of life and dominant cultural trends centred around certain products. Advertising must rearrange value systems — even ultimate values — so that these are compatible with the production, marketing and consumption of these products. Once major institutions are adjusted and cultural norms established, the influence on our way of perceiving the world is indirect. We need never watch television or read popular magazines. The myths that new products mean progress, better health, more happiness become the 'normal' meaning of life. Those who think that they are above the 'cult of consumerism' may be the most deluded. Not even the contemplative hermit is completely immune from the dominant world-view of a society.[9]

The influence of the media is inescapable; but what is the extent of its effect? Individuals and groups may not be able to avoid it, but they might be able to learn how to defend themselves to a degree against it. From time to time it is suggested that Churches could become counter-cultural bodies in which such resistance would be strengthened. They would then, so the argument goes, become the source of lively criticism of the media, and so agents of change or a bulwark against an influence which is presumed to be malign.

An example of this stance is the Television Awareness Training Programme which the Media Action Resource Center has produced in the United States. In the United Kingdom the Mothers' Union is sponsoring similar efforts. Through T–A–T individuals, families and church groups have their awareness of what may be happening to them aroused. They thus learn to erect defences against the intrusion of the mass media. The programme seems to benefit the participants. Its long-term effect remains to be assessed.

Such training, however, is domestic to the Churches and their members and friends. By changing their perceptions and sensitivity they hope to alter their immediate environment. For church leaders, however, the question remains whether the form of the Church itself should include a publicly critical role in relation to the media. For any such task, a clear notion of the extensial dimension to the mass media is essential.

This, however, is not at present easy to determine. Since the media in their present form are so recent an invention, this is an issue that the Churches' ministers will need to hold in mind and about which they will have to create hypotheses with no guarantee of a conclusion for some time to come.

The extensial question impinges directly on ecclesiology. Present trends in every Church seem to be toward assessing its life and activity by reference to its members' behaviour and their spiritual and pastoral achievements. This, however, may be part of the pressure towards the immediate that is a symptom of the new age of communications. It could, however, be that Churches, and especially their ministers, need a deeper sense not so much of the immediate as of the proximate—that which Churches believe on behalf of others.[10] Once again, therefore, the theme of the nature of the Church, its task and the roles of its ministers, is exposed by attention to an issue which arises less from the content of media productions than from the fact of their existence.

CONCLUSION

Each of these areas, the managerial, the evidential, the moral and the extensial, is a dimension of life in our contemporary society which is made explicit by the media. The questions which we have begun to note about their functioning are not confined to media or communications studies. They are also major issues for those engaged in theological education.

The strength of considering such apparently intractable issues by reference to the media, is that they become locatable enough to be discussed in relation to an experienced reality. It is not possible to escape either into theory or into a self-chosen definition (and in all probability a narrow view) of the world. Because 'media' are indefinable and so obviously pervasive, when we work with them we find what we oscillate between the examination of cases in everyday life and theoretical formulations. In other words, we work through testable hypotheses. This specifically means moving between the experience of Christian living and its demands and the vastness of the resource of the gospel. There is no escape for ministers from this process of interpretation as we learn about ministry. But that is only to be expected; for the same process is the foundation of the practice of Christian ministry. The style of learning and the application in practice thus become congruent.

Notes

1. E. R. Shapiro and A. W. Carr, *Lost in Familiar Places: The Interpretation of Experience from Family to Society* (Princeton and London, Yale University Press, 1990/1 forthcoming).

2. M. Muggeridge, *Christ and the Media* (London, Hodder & Stoughton, 1977).

3. Plato, *Republic*, 10.606d.

4. Fore, *Television and Religion*, p. 143. See generally chapters 9 and 10.

5. David Hay, *Exploring Inner Space* (Harmondsworth, Pelican, 1982).

6. e.g. C. J. Arthur, *In the Hall of Mirrors: Problems of Commitment in a Religiously Plural World* (Oxford, Mowbrays, 1986).

7. Wolfe, *Churches and BBC*, pp. 3–133.

8. See the essays in G. Comstock, ed., *Public Communication and Behavior*, vol. 1 (Orlando, Academic Press, 1986), especially William J. McGuire, 'The Myth of Massive Media Impact: Savagings and Salvagings'.

9. *Communication Research Trends* (1982), vol. 3, p. 1.

10. See, for instance, Bruce Reed, *The Dynamics of Religion* (London, Darton, Longman & Todd, 1978); Carr, *The Priestlike Task*; and John Habgood, *Church and Nation in a Secular Age* (London, Darton, Longman & Todd, 1983).

5 THE MEDIA AND MINISTRY

Each of the four issues which are raised by media-saturation —
the managerial, the evidential, the moral and the extensial — is
also significant for religious belief and for the practice of
ministry.

LOCATING MYSELF IN THE WORLD

The *managerial issue* is chiefly about how I locate myself in the
world. The existential question, which underlies much religious
belief and aspiration — 'Who am I?' — may be asked and heard as
self-centred. But in daily living it emerges as a question about
the relation between myself and my various contexts and how
this is negotiated or, we might say, mediated. Individual identity
cannot be divorced from the interchange between the given self
and the discovered self. Personal individuality arises within
contexts, not in isolation.

Birth and growth provide an illustration. The new-born child
is an individual in his or her own right only when thought of in
relation to the mother from whom he or she has been born. Our
fused closeness with mother and developing separation from her
as we grow both contribute to who we are. Our individuality is
generated as we relate to our parents. This process continues
throughout life and needs managing by all involved. The
managerial question of how I locate myself in the world from
birth and continue to do so through life concerns my personal
identity and is profoundly theological.

The media face us with our cultural context. In a pluralist
society, where values, rituals and symbols are less uniform than
they once were, the problem of context is correspondingly more
acute. We become daily more aware of the variety and number of
contexts within which we have to locate ourselves. These are
precisely the points where conflict and contention arise. The

perennial question of how we are to manage our personal identity is complicated by that of how we conceive the identity of the culture in which we live and to which we contribute.

Modern theological education offers an illuminating instance of this dilemma. Ministerial training today is more practically oriented than it was believed to have been formerly. I emphasize 'was believed to have been' because this comparison with the past is usually made without reference to the changing social environment. Training programmes usually include at least one placement, and usually a series. Students are sent to parishes, churches or other institutions for periods. There they are expected to study how ministry is offered and to learn something of the cultural context within which they will minister through being exposed to living and working in those environments. This development in the curriculum is in part a response to the perceived need for theological education to be both specific and yet profound enough to sustain a minister throughout a lifetime's ministry. To do this he or she requires a sense of the potential variety of contexts in which that ministry will be exercised.

But the vogue for placements involves a serious error: it reduces the notion of 'context' to that of 'place'. Students' experiences on these placements vary. The pressures that they feel may be socially rather than intellectually stretching. The setting is usually selected as different from that with which the student is familiar. The parish or institution is frequently considered 'difficult' or 'exciting'; the ministers and other leaders are people of obvious ability. They naturally engender admiration for their ministry; but the consequent impairment of the students' critical faculties may be underestimated.

This occurs because the student, however much invited to participate, remains an observer and his or her immersion in the prevailing culture is less than intended. As a result reflection and learning about oneself and about the gospel in their common cultural context are both diminished. Yet everywhere present but in this approach overlooked are the media, which constitute the major *cultural* phenomenon of the age. When we grasp this point, it is possible, as we shall see, to transform the sound, but flawed, theory behind placements into effective learning for pastoral and preaching ministry.

But to make this step we must go further. The managerial

issue also draws attention to an aspect of the individual that can be overlooked or even undervalued in a training programme. People who use religious language are prone to speak casually of persons and personhood. Study of personal growth is regularly included in contemporary pastoral learning. For theological thinking, however, this idea is too vague. It falls noticeably short when we consider vocation. When we talk of vocation to some ministry we are not speaking about individuals as persons. We are describing a possible transition from one role to another. For instance, when John's vocation to the priesthood is affirmed by selection and ordination, John remains John. There is, however, a shift in one of the many roles that are his: the layman John gives place to the ordained John. The precise nature of the change does not concern us here. The crucial unquestioned fact is that he assumes a new role and surrenders an old one.

Like any other transition in life, this one needs managing. The moment, therefore, we reflect on the media and the way in which they require us to attend to the managerial issue that they bring to prominence, we inevitably have also to consider a similar area which lies at the heart of the religious life—changes of role and their management. Talk of human beings can become very general. Discussion of role, by contrast, must be specific. And the roles in question are not restricted to one or two, such as those of the lay person or the ordained. There is an almost infinite series of other roles that come in for consideration.

The experience of being so lost in familiar places directs us to the heart of the religious life: myself and my roles within the divine order. 'How will I manage myself in the dilemmas of human existence?' This question makes us face ourselves; and it demands that we examine our contexts. Ministers, therefore, must have some clarity about it, if they are to exercise a ministry. Attention to the media and its cultural functioning will locate both trainee and experienced ministers precisely in one area where they must be, if they are to be effective.

SPEAKING OF THE UNKNOWABLE

The second issue was *evidential*. In the case of media studies this question was about how we might assess influence, what would constitute evidence and how we could evaluate it. The dimension of this issue which concerns theology lies in the field of the philosophy of religion. How may we speak of the unknowable? How may we identify the ways of God? What constitutes evidence? How do we evaluate competing claims? The minister cannot escape these and similar questions.

It is important to note how philosophical teaching has declined in today's theological education. For example, of the students on the Project a few possessed some philosophy from earlier degree courses. But most lacked any such training. The main exception is the syllabus at the Roman Catholic seminaries, which includes philosophy as a major component. Although during training most of the students had not been wholly enthusiastic, more than one commented when at work in parishes that it was the ability to think philosophically that became a pastoral mainstay. The same point was separately endorsed by an Anglican ordinand who happened to have studied philosophy.

In the previous chapter a central problem was about what would be evidence for the extent of the media's influence. The same issue arises about the place and function of religion in a secular society. We are mostly at a loss to know how to test the extent of the Churches' influence. There are two sides to this. One is familiar; it has to do with the intellectual climate of the age. We are still faced with the philosophical question of what such influence would be and what would demonstrate God's activity with men and women. Obviously fundamental, this problem is not new. It has been and remains central to any religious faith.

Today's new difficulty occurs at an apparently simpler level, which proves more complex. Sociological approaches to religion prove too imprecise for those who are members of, and are to minister in, the Churches. It is hard to discover what data are relevant to a particular issue, how we are to acquire them, order them, evaluate them and consequently act upon them. If such study is restricted to the actual Churches, what then happens to the range of religious belief that suffuses society but which lacks, and maybe does not for the most part seek, specific expression? Such questions are serious for ministers, not only because they impinge on their perspective on ministry but because they also affect the first set of questions, those which have traditionally comprised the study of the philosophy of religion. The problem, therefore, is not simply solved by the reintroduction of the study of philosophy. Equally, however, extended courses in the sociology of religion are unlikely to be adequately earthed for the student to be able to learn.

These difficulties are not purely educational. They lie at the heart of a teaching and pastoral ministry. In any encounter pastors will, usually without much time for reflection, have to assess what they are being presented with and what data they judge to be central and what peripheral. They will then have to put them together as a hypothesis as the basis on which to try and respond to those with whom they are dealing. Having done all this, so far as they are able, they will then have to determine a course of action which is sufficiently congruent with the presenting issues and with their own awareness of their role as pastor, priest or minister.[1]

This is the evidential problem with which the media confront us in a particular form. The Churches' discussions about media influence should no longer be confined to questions of the media or communications' studies alone. The issues need to be extrapolated to the wider areas of contemporary life that are being indicated here. They may then become an entry point for ministers, through which they can begin to examine philosophical enquiry and learning as well as the practical concerns of applied pastoralia.

We should not, however, lose sight of another dimension of learning, to which consideration of the evidential question directs us. It may be, as was hinted by the students' experience, that there should be a larger philosophical component in the curriculum for contemporary theological education. Many British philosophers have recently been preoccupied with language. At first sight there may seem to be neat links between this and our primary concern with communication. But in practice this offers no way forward. John Kelly has shown that any attempt to link the study of philosophy with that of communication requires a philosophy of communication itself, not just of language, and in today's world this can only be done on a phenomenological basis.

> To analyse the world of daily life philosophically is to begin to differentiate one's consciousness. That is to say, it is to begin to be aware of and to recognize different forms or modes of human knowing and, consequently, of human communication. . . . Differentiated

consciousnesses are not common. Yet today, when we are inundated with views, opinions, convictions of all shapes, sizes and colours (conveyed to us by highly sophisticated means), the differentiation of consciousness is urgently necessary. Undifferentiated consciousness is likely to result in an inert, unquestioning, stagnant common sense which can infect all other modes of human knowing . . . That is why, *in any overall plan for safeguarding communication, I see as fundamental, re-education in a proper method of knowing.*[2]

There are major questions, therefore, to be placed against the lack of philosophical study, as outlined in this quotation, in contemporary theological education. It is no use, however, proposing that there should be more. That would be to put another burden on burdened teachers and stress on stressed syllabuses. But the use of the media as a focus for a coherent curriculum could in principle provide a ground for more philosophical learning, using the evidential issue and its significance for communication as the key.

THE STUDY OF ETHICS

The third and fourth issues raised by the media can be dealt with more swiftly. The third, the *moral dimension,* would seem undoubtedly one where media concerns and religious question coincide. Morals and ethics remain crucial areas of religious life. If in belief we begin to face the existential question of who I am, the parallel step must be to ask what am I for and how am I to live. The importance of moral questioning is self-evident.

It is, therefore, an intriguing piece of history to note that some years ago for a period the General Ordination Examination of the Church of England did not include a paper on ethics. This odd state of affairs was rectified, but it produced a generation of clergy who were ignorant in a vital area of ministry. Ethical problems are probably the most commonplace and significant that clergy encounter. When approached for counsel they are usually being invited to provide some sort of moral guidance.

Participants in the Project, during their first year of public ministry reported without exception that they found themselves unexpectedly required to discuss and advise on moral questions. The demand for guidance has not changed, so much as what is done with it. People today seek assistance against a background of a strange sense of autonomy. They thus appear to be selective in their response rather than obedient. So while it sometimes looks as though the authority of the clergy has declined, or even disappeared, it does not follow that what they are required to represent or offer has been abandoned.

The connections between moral problems and the mass media are many. We have already discussed some of the more obvious questions, especially that of authority. This is perhaps the major point at which the media impinge on ministry. In a confusing world, people are tempted to seek simple responses to the dilemmas which they feel are becoming increasingly complex. The adage that 'a little knowledge is a dangerous thing' becomes more true as people acquire pieces of unconnected information through the media at the very time that they are losing confidence in any source of authority.

One resulting pressure on ministers is to become simplistic. On the Project this was experientially confirmed. When faced on the media with moral stances with which they felt uncomfortable or at odds, the students, whatever their background or denomination, instinctively found that a 'Muggeridgean' stance of despair or flight became attractive. Only critical reflection showed them what was happening.

Church councils and leaders from time to time manifest the same behaviour. But the complexity of moral life is relentlessly reproduced on the radio or television, and ministers, if they are to work with people in this environment, will have to develop a way of moral thinking which can lead to guidance. John Habgood has outlined what is required:

> The search for moral guidance in such a world is admittedly complex, but absolutism and emotivism are not the only alternatives. Moral insights are neither given nor merely invented. In many fields of human life they have to be won painfully, by reflection on Scripture, by attention to tradition, by absorption of the best available knowledge, by a process of trial and error, and by the exercise of creative imagination.[3]

MINISTRY TO INDEFINABLE EXPECTATIONS

The fourth and final aspect was that for which the word *extensial* was offered: is there any means by which we can determine limits to media influence? While difficult to define precisely, this criterion proves surprisingly important as an indicator for ministry. It draws our attention away from individuals, their beliefs and needs, to institutions and their functioning.

Few ministers are in their posts for long before discovering that they are the focus of hitherto undiscerned expectations from people who explicitly, and sometimes blatantly, do not associate with their church. Even small gathered Churches in the Free Church tradition find a discrepancy between the numbers who claim association and the numbers who attend. For some Churches, for example the Church of England, it is a specific ecclesiological problem which perpetually raises issues about the nature of the institutional Church. Around every religious institution there is a penumbra of religiosity, for which it is a focus and which it also engenders. Yet it is difficult to find a way to approach this phenomenon which does not lead either to the delusions of ministerial anecdotes or the aridity of sociological survey.

Using the problem as it is perceived through the media could be a way of tangentially approaching this central issue for working churches and ministers. It will be recalled that the extensial question, when addressed to the media, cannot yet be answered, even though its importance is acknowledged. So for the present it is an issue which needs to be held in mind but which cannot lead to a conclusion. It thus becomes a referent by which to ensure that problematic questions are not obliterated, not least because of the discomfort they generate.

That is exactly the stance about the extensial influence of the Church that is required of the Churches' ministers, especially in their role as leaders. Without it, the nature of the Church as an institution will be falsely perceived, with consequentially problematic outcomes. Recognition of the media and the extensial dimension to the issues they raise would at least hold the problem in the mind of those who are thinking about the Church and their future ministry in a way which would allow critical study and expansive questioning. Such institutional awareness coupled with critical use of the imagination is another vital component in ministry.

THE FOUR ISSUES AND CHRISTIAN THEOLOGY

In sum, therefore, those issues which we saw to be raised by our living in a media-saturated environment also lie at the heart of the questions with which religion deals. Even in a secular world, Churches are still expected to handle them. But practical approaches are not enough. These questions also require theological exploration. So finally we may indicate what might be the significance of these perspectives for Christian theology.

The managerial issue points to the Christian questions of conversion and belief. When we talk about the self, which self are we discussing? And in particular, what or who is the Christian self who becomes the person of faith and commitment? Self management, the core problem raised by the managerial demands of the media, is not simply a human question. It is also central to Christian faith.

Turning to the second, the evidential question, we are directed to doctrine. The nature and content of belief, its relation to the tradition of faith, and the reasonableness of belief are all matters which lie at the heart of the Christian faith and life. They are consequently required fields of study for those who are to be the Churches' ministers.

Thirdly, the moral dimension encourages reflection on behaviour and specifically whether there is any longer a distinctively Christian ethic. It is worth noting that in practice this question often surfaces in direct relation to the media culture. For instance, what is the appropriate Christian witness in the face of conspicuous consumption and its advocacy? Or again, is there a Christian response to the persistent presentation of, and invited participation in, violence? Or, perhaps even more difficult, in the light of the documentaries which bring the world into our homes, what is the moral basis, if any, of Christian missionary activity?

Finally we come up against the extensial problem of the nature of the Christian Church and its relation to the world. The necessary uncertainty of the answer to any question about extent of influence militates against implicit triumphalism and against simplistic answers to the Churches' place in society. Although the impact of a media-saturated society seems implicitly to encourage the idea of individual autonomy, the relevance of institutions and their functioning is brought to prominence.

CONCLUSION

Thus at this theoretical level, attention to the media and their cultural aspects, even when we grant that they cannot be precisely defined and may be only cursorily explored, brings us to the heart of Christian belief and theology. We, therefore, find ourselves traversing a familiar route but with unfamiliar perspectives on it. We have here the beginnings of an agenda for reconsidering ministry which could be strong. For it links facets, possibly all of them, of contemporary society, culture and individual life with fundamental theological issues. None of these can be resolved merely by acquiring skills. We are, therefore, spared that facile response, not least in any thinking about the media, where preoccupation with techniques has restricted thinking. At the same time, there can be no flight into some idealized form of theology, whether conservative or liberal. The four areas, discerned in the impact of the media and confirmed as central for religion and specifically for the Christian Church, can form the ground for a genuine practical theology. For the test of that is how communicable is everything that is thought, prayed and preached, as well as learned.

Notes

1. Carr, *The Priestlike Task.*

2. John C. Kelly, *A Philosophy of Communication* (London, The Centre for the Study of Communications and Culture, 1981), pp. 7f, italics mine.

3. John Habgood, *Confessions of A Conservative Liberal* (London, SPCK, 1989), p. 142.

6 TRIVIALIZING GOD?

When the Project was initially being established, teachers and students persistently expressed the same anxiety. Since the mass media trivialize everything, will they not have the same effect on theological education and the Churches' ministry? Their nervousness is understandable and a salutary warning to anyone thinking about Church, religion, theology and the media. Any curriculum which used only the output of the media as input for learning would rapidly become frivolous. But this outcome is not inevitable. Indeed, as we have seen, careful reflection on the media culture will, if we will allow it, lead us directly to key questions of religious faith and practice.

The participants, first as students and later as newly ordained ministers, reflected on their learning and ministerial practice. They were also asked deliberately to reflect upon their lives in other roles as citizens, parents, husbands, wives, etc. From these twin perspectives, five basic points repeatedly emerged. On what happened to these, so it appeared, the future of the Churches' ministry depends.

THE SURVIVAL OF IMAGINATION

When we think of how the mass media may be affecting us and our children, immediately we think of imagination. What may be happening to people's imagination and their capacity to use it? To some extent this looks like a generational question. Parents who were themselves children before the advent of television (or at least when television was beginning to be widespread) may be more affected by it and concerned about its effect than their children, who have been raised with it as part of everyday life. But there is a continuing unease that exposure to the mass media may stultify our imagination or change the way in which it functions.

It is unlikely that such questions can be confidently answered. But that does not prevent them being asked. There has long been an obvious connection between religion, art and imagination. Research into the beliefs and capacity for belief in teenagers, for example, confirms the central significance of imagination.

> Spiritual growth in the individual is often dependent on his or her finding a means of expression—verbal or symbolic—which will enable him or her to bring into consciousness and reflect upon what otherwise might remain intangible or disappear, perhaps for ever.[1]

Imagination is not merely an internal capacity. If it is to be used in their development, people seem to need means of articulating what they imagine. Mere telling, however, is not enough. For when we try to put imaginative thoughts into formal sentences, most of us find that they are diminished to extinction. In practice, therefore, we use such available symbols as we can find to be our means of expression. Notable among these, and of immediate relevance to religious people, are rituals and liturgies.

When publicly available and socially legitimate rituals lose their efficacy, for whatever reason, it does not follow that ritual declines into irrelevance or disappears. Robert Bocock, for example, disclosed such rituals in industrial society. Although allowance would now have to be made for the changes in industry since he wrote (in 1974), nevertheless his work demonstrated the principle.[2] More recently Gregor Goethals has pointed out the impact of political ritual on the complex pluralism of the United States.[3]

For the theologian there is also sophisticated reflection on imagination. Wolfhart Pannenberg compares our capacity for imaginative thinking with the function of instinct in animals. Imagination is not just desirable; we require it for survival. In other words, atrophy of the imagination is not a possibly unfortunate development. If it happens, human beings will cease to be human and could cease to exist.[4]

No theological student can ignore these questions of religion, art and their place in human development; ritual and the way that it functions as people orient themselves in the world; or the capacity for imagination, upon which our survival seems to depend. Whatever the exact statistical and technical discoveries that are made about the impact of the mass media, there is no doubt that they explicitly affect each of these areas. Indeed, since they specifically operate in the realms of fantasy and imagination, they must be altering our perception of the nature of life and the interpretation of its meaning. In that sense the media can never be peripheral to theology. Not only do they raise such questions; they also provide a defined forum in which they can be addressed.

TRANSCENDENCE

The idea of transcendence is closely linked with this issue of the capacity to imagine. When we speak of 'transcendence' we affirm that to every human situation there is a larger referent, even if it is not always apparent. Each moment or each context appears incomplete. Sensing this we come face to face with the awesomeness of life.

Religious people quickly slide into describing this sense of otherness, awe or strangeness, as 'God'. But such a leap is too superficial, especially for someone who is to minister to others. Some may find it easy to make the identification. But many, including religious believers, cannot accept that this jump is legitimate. Transcendence is a central issue of life and a key dimension for religion, but the two are not identical. We have already mentioned studies which have demonstrated that the sense of transcendence remains widespread even in a secular society. The problem, however, is whether this is in spite of or because of the media culture.

As an example we may consider the difficulty now facing teachers of religious education. Chris Arthur has suggested that we are suffering from 'transcendence blindness', a condition in which our sensitivity to significance declines because we are progressively losing contact with the elemental facts of life and associated religious ideas. He cites Peter Berger's observation that 'modern society has banished the night from consciousness so far as this is possible', and further comments:

> The bulk of TV . . . looks out from a spiritual wilderness and presents this as a true picture of how things are. As such, it constitutes a formidable barrier to effective religious education.[5]

Yet the sense of transcendence (not just the idea) persists. Although possibly diminished, from time to time it surfaces and becomes a key theological and pastoral concern. Yet precisely because of the ease with which he or she is likely to speak of 'God' and 'transcendence', the assumptive world of the media is a valuable context within which the theologian can examine aspects of experience. Indeed, if Arthur and others are correct and this side of human life is declining in immediacy, then it is all the more essential that theologians and pastors should consider this fact carefully. For if some sense of transcendence sustains believing ministers in their role, then, unless it is earthed in the contemporary world, it will not be a reference point for interpretation of life with others.

PERSONALITY AND RELATIONSHIPS

The theme of transcendence leads naturally to the third area of major importance: what it is to be human. This sort of question is an enlargement of the more narrow one about a transcendent dimension to existence. Awareness of people and their humanity was one of the most live issues during the work of the Project. The participants found that their sensitivity and alertness to everyday human life was intensified by their conscious thinking about the media. The reason is obvious: a mark of the media is their cult of the personality. Shows are named after individuals and celebrities are created and destroyed. Like mayflies they have their day of glory and depart. Because of this, there is an implicit, and insidiously effective, re-ordering of priorities in life.

For example, on 21 January 1989 *The Boston Globe* reported the inauguration of George Bush as President of the United States. Underneath a large colour picture on the front page a note ran: 'Text of speech: page 8. How TV handled the inauguration: page 7.' Before we could read and think about what the new President had to say to the nation and the world, we were regaled with reports and evaluations of how the personalities on the various channels comported themselves during the day.

But while we may regret, and sometimes mock, this promotion of personalities and the associated distortions, the cult of the individual is a steady reminder that concern with human life, values and interests is central to all the media. They may from time to time drift into prurience, but overall they consistently hold up before a large audience other people, their behaviour, their views, their eccentricities, their heroism and so on. Television in particular is about talk and human intercourse, stressing relationships between people on the screen and between those on the screen and those off, the personalities and the viewers.

It would be naive to laud this as something profoundly significant. Story-tellers have long known that people are intrigued by people. The relationship between the teller and the audience, once this is through technology and the screen, is more complex than hitherto but substantially no different. Even so, there was a time when some commentators seemed to think that television would confirm the modern 'tribal group', the family. The whole family was expected to sit down together each night and share a common pursuit and discussion about it. This proved a forlorn hope; people are not like that.

Nevertheless, it is important to observe that the media, for all their influence, even dominance, in people's lives, stand less for wondrous technology than for the centrality of human relations. They implicitly keep prominent a series of primary questions about people, which are also theological: What is the significance of human relations? How are they generated, sustained and ended? Do we treat each other well enough?

For the religious person—and in particular for the theologically informed—the presentation of these issues, from the news to soap opera, arouses curiosity about the meaning of love. And after a moment's reflection the Christian will realize that there are here also indicators of the nature of incarnation. Belief in the willingness of God himself to be trivialized and to surrender control in his relationship with his creation lies at the core of this Christian belief. This topic, too, is daily presented in the media. For whatever else the programmes and publications may do, they do not allow abstraction. Anyone invited to contribute to any programme soon discovers this. Presentations have to be concrete, not abstract. It is at this point that reflection and the acquisition of media skills, which, while not the most important matter, is nevertheless desirable in this age, come together.

THE PERSISTENCE OF MEMORY

A fourth key human issue which is raised when we attend to the media is memory. This caused more discussion and possibly anxiety than any other single concern during the Project work. In part this may be because the exercise of memory is an essential characteristic of religious practice and therefore vital for the capacity for believing. Hence whenever memory is challenged, people feel that the foundations of their faith are being assaulted. Each believer has his or her own pilgrimage which is constructed on remembered experience. They recall whence they came, so that they can discover what is required of them now and whither they are going. This is one reason for the perennial attractiveness of Bunyan's *Pilgrim's Progress*. The hero, Christian, progresses with an accumulation of memories as he matures and journeys towards the promised land.

Parallel with individual pilgrimage, and from time to time coinciding with it, is the corporate memory of the body of believers, the Church. Scripture and tradition ought to become a dead weight. Yet they remain living forces because they form the connection of memories. Our memory does not run in a straight line. Remembering changes the way we view time and therefore our sense of progress through life. Our journey is not from beginning to end. It has more the quality of dreams. We make links back and forth as different remembrances are revived and die.

The liturgy is designed to represent such corporate memory. Both Passover and Eucharist are characterized by conscious addressing of collective memory. 'We', when spoken or thought, cannot be restricted to those present but includes the enlarged company, before and since, of which our momentary 'we' is part. It is a religious idea that memories from the past, however long ago, can be regenerated in the present and there have an energizing effect.

The new media seem to be bringing about a fundamental shift in memory. One symptom of this is the way in which the word itself is given new usage. Computers are measured by their 'memory' and electronic devices, such as video recorders or telephones, are sold by the capacity of their 'memory'. Memory becomes technical as recording becomes more easily available. Subtly, therefore, it is shifting from being a key function of our humanity, and of religious activity in particular, to becoming a problem of technology.

Parallel to this development, although as yet the connection remains unproved, people seem to find it less necessary to develop their ability to remember what they have learned. Educationalists argue over this issue and changes seem inevitable. But alert believers may already ask themselves what the consequences will be if memory is relegated to technology and remembering as a human activity is minimized.

One result is that people seem to become more reliant on sources outside themselves for information. A computer, for example, can provide any amount of data, but it is unlikely to place the operator in his or her historical context. It might, therefore, follow that Churches may be thought of as memory banks for certain types of memory and in particular for their quality. They then become places (or better, institutions) to which people turn when they want to locate and gain access to a certain sort of memory. To some extent Churches already perform this function. The memory, for example, of war may be located in a religious place—a church, a laid-up flag or a cenotaph. Memory of how to behave—the idea of what is 'correct' or 'proper'—seems still to be held by church rituals. Even when these are not observed, they are assumed to carry value. Rituals around birth, less so marriage, but certainly death are still held by the Church but not owned by it. Many a pastor has been bewildered by the response to his question as to why people have come for a wedding: 'It's the proper thing to do.' And new secular rituals owe much to their church origins.[6]

There is, therefore, an observable connection between theology, pastoral practice and the effect of the media when we consider memory. Inevitably changes of this type are slow and not easy to discern with certainty. Arguments, therefore, necessarily become speculative. This, however, should not prevent them occurring, especially in the education of those who are to be the Churches' ministers. Change in the concept of memory may be among the most significant factors in the contemporary media revolution. If so, theology is bound to be profoundly affected. We can offer an example.

Tradition at the moment presents the Churches with a difficulty. The arguments about the importance that it is to be assigned to ecclesiology are being revived in ecumenical discussion and practice. Whenever invoked it frequently becomes a point of conflict rather than of growth. In part this is a result of a model of tradition which is marked by accumulation. An institution, in this case a Church, acquires more and more facets of life which are enshrined as 'traditional' simply because they have occurred. Some theologians, however, have realized that in practice tradition functions more dynamically than this. They propound an artistic model. Something less tangible can be found to have direct connection with its past but at the same time to create something new. The work of a pupil artist is the pattern: however original in itself, it will display the skill learned from the master.[7]

But this notion has yet to surface effectively within living Churches, where it could be a liberating concept. For the moment such thinking has limited effect because it originates among academic theologians, whose views are not highly regarded. An instance of the difficulties that such assumptions cause may be seen in the struggles of the Bishop of Durham (David Jenkins) in the 1980s. The impact of the media on the nature of memory, however, may stimulate this important debate in the Churches.

EXPERIENCE AND RELIGIOUS BELIEF

The fourth topic which regularly emerges in reflection on the media concerns the nature of experience and its relation to religious belief. One effect of the modern media is that we are more self-conscious about our experience. In any discussion of this topic it is impossible with any certainty to distinguish cause from effect: are we more self-conscious because of the nature of our experience? Or is the perceived nature of our experience the effect of our being more self-conscious? Whatever the case, it is difficult to disentangle the media's impact in this respect from other attitudes and assumptions which have developed in the post-Freudian era. However, the consistent public probing of people, based largely on a sceptical stance, and the way in which people's foibles are relentlessly exposed by the media, may affect our sense of what constitutes experience. People compare themselves with those they see and of whom they hear. This observation returns us to the familiar problem of the extent to which people's behaviour is directly influenced by what is shown on the screen.

One outcome is anxiety about privacy. The British are said to be naturally reticent, although such generalizations are questionable when cross-sections of this 'reticent' populace appear on television for their fifteen minutes of fame. But anxiety about privacy and exposure, together with fear of contravening cultural norms, which are only media presentations, is liable to distort the way in which people communicate with one another.

As a result of these twin pressures—exposure and desire for privacy—the communication of experience becomes a problem in a new way. It has never been easy. But it has been possible to believe that people can share a common experience and reflect on it together. Today we are more aware of the difficulties and the study of human behaviour looks set to continue to affirm such doubt. At the intellectual level this can be the subject of enquiry and debate. In everyday life doubt gives way to pragmatism. People operate on the assumption that they can and do share. But this state of affairs may not survive for long. For the more the process of communication is publicly discussed as a problem, whether in documentaries or in the everyday *Angst* of soap operatic life, the more the question of communicating something as intangible as belief will become acute. Communication is apparently becoming more complicated as we study it.

But we should also note the deleterious effects. For we do not hold attitudes to communicating experience as if they lay outside us when we watch the screen or listen to the loudspeaker. They are part of ourselves, as a result of which we become unsure about what is actually of us and what is not. The boundary of the self becomes unclear, especially when we consider the experience of interpersonal communication. Then, being less confident that we 'know' our own experience, we become less willing to risk whatever we consider it to be with others. Thus people's reticence to talk about anything unusual, especially religious or transcendent experience, is confirmed.

Only those who are oblivious to these problems or insensitive to others persist in the blasé assumption that communication is merely a matter of getting the technique right or the voice loud enough. Yet churchpeople need to be sensitive to their prejudices in this area, as well as to remember that many people's experience of religious communication derives from groups which adopt such stances. For the moment in Great Britain they are heard in

90

the streets. In the United States they have reached the screen. This is a crucial area for ministry. It is not just a matter of television and 'tele-evangelists' but of the possibilities for ministers of their communicating with anyone, whether through preaching, liturgy or pastoring.

CONCLUSION

One small piece of evidence from the Project illustrates what has been argued in this chapter. Each group of students, whatever their theological and denominational background, *without exception* noted that, as they became more alert to the media and issues of communication, they also became more acutely aware of their personal spiritual lives, their internal selves and the presence of that 'other' — their neighbour.

This observation provides yet another link between ministry, theology and the media. This sort of two-directional learning is precisely the ideal of 'formation'. It emphasizes both the minister's representative role and his or her internal (or personal) ordering. In other words, since one inevitable role of ministers is to represent the Church, its message and gospel, they are obviously concerned with communications. But since they are also expected to be models, they must be people whose personal spirituality is explorable by any who approach or look to them.

Formation includes the notion of integration: coherence between the self with the message, or, in more familiar language, the role and the person. There is, however, one further dimension — the interpersonal aspect to living. In this discussion, we have seen how this, too, is set in a specific context and as a result becomes explorable and testable, rather than remaining merely an ideal. The media-saturated culture and the Christian tradition may at many points be in conflict. Nevertheless, by bringing them together in programmes of theological education, we can see how the partnership can also be creative for contemporary theology as well as for learning and pastoral practice.

Notes

1. Edward Robinson and Michael Jackson, *Religious Values at Sixteen Plus* (Oxford, Alister Hardy Research Centre, 1987), p. 65.

2. R. J. Bocock, *Ritual in Industrial Society* (London, George Allen & Unwin, 1974).

3. Goethals, *TV Ritual*.

4. Wolfhart Pannenberg, *Anthropology in a Theological Perspective* (Edinburgh, T. & T. Clark, 1985), pp. 377ff.

5. Arthur, 'Television, Transcendence and Religious Education', p. 1. The reference is to Peter Berger, *A Rumour of Angels: Modern Society and the Rediscovery of the Supernatural* (Harmondsworth, Penguin, 1971), p. 95.

6. Wesley Carr, *Brief Encounters: Pastoral Ministry through the Occasional Offices* (London, SPCK, 1985).

7. Christopher Evans, 'The Christian Past—Tradition', in *Explorations in Theology 2* (London, SCM, 1977), pp. 141ff.

7 RELEVANCE AND IDENTITY

We turn now to a critical theme for ministry: the balance between relevance and identity. When communication is considered, among the questions that arise are some about the person who is attempting to communicate. This is also true of the gospel. When we pause to think about how it is to be communicated, we discover that it is constantly disclosed at points of interaction. These may be between Church and world, or Christian and neighbour, or believer and God. The exact place makes little difference and depends upon circumstances. But as soon as the identity of one party is affirmed, questions of relevance of the other emerge. And as we negotiate all these relationships and struggle with issues of relevance and identity, there the gospel is discerned.

This is the central problem facing the Church, which lives between the demand that it should be relevant to changing cultures and its own need to sustain sufficient identity in order to remain faithful to its origins.[1] This is not only for the benefit of its members, but also so that it can be identifiable by others as and when they need it.

Relevance and identity are a specific theme in theological education, from which illustrations in this chapter are drawn. But although the discussion uses the training of ordinands for its specific instances, as indicated earlier, the whole range of Christian learning for ministry is also implicitly included. The chapter also temporarily leaves media issues in order to describe the particular function which they can most usefully perform in the training and sustaining of the Church's ministers.

INTEGRATED MINISTERS

Many students experience their training as a series of fragments. Sometimes these have tenuous links with each other; at other times the pieces seem unconnected. Teachers likewise struggle to conceive an agreed, unifying stance towards the components of the course. In general individuals are expected to achieve whatever degree of integration they can attain. They are offered opportunities for learning and given supervision. Tutors help order personal, spiritual and social development. The ideal is that eventually they should emerge from this process as those who have integrated themselves and their learning and are capable of exercising a ministry. Integration is central to theological education; it is also a core topic for the life of the Church and its ministers.

Many students achieve a preliminary level of integration. But even the most experienced minister will wonder whether he or she, after years of practice, has made further progress. The reason for this seems to be that because they are required to achieve this integration themselves, they are likely to do it to their own satisfaction. As a consequence, whether wittingly or not, they make selections, ignoring that which induces stress and emphasizing that which is congenial. There is nothing strange in this: it is normal human behaviour. But it is a serious deficiency in ministers. Practical problems are not the core issue. We can note three major factors:

THE DIFFICULTIES IN ACHIEVING INTEGRATION

(a) Personal Disarray

One function of a sound programme of education is to induce personal disarray. The limitations and inaccuracies in previous knowledge have to be exposed and bold ideas have to be explored. New knowledge, new styles of thinking and new levels of argument should all do their subversive work.

But theological learning is designed not only to challenge the mind, but also to throw the heart (or soul) into turmoil. This process cannot be engineered, although it might be manipulated. But since cherished beliefs, which themselves have constituted the minister's motivations are themselves under question by the educational process, the student should undergo a process of especially profound disturbance, challenge, disarray and hopefully in the end change. A familiar example is the effect on those from conservative backgrounds when for the first time they encounter the critical approach to Scripture. Another occurs when devout Catholics discover that there are other views of history and tradition than those which imbue them. And for everyone, whatever their background, the philosophical questioning of belief, practice and doctrine will have an impact upon the prayer and spiritual activities which sustain the religious life.

(b) The Fantasized Context

Vocational training, including that for ordination, takes place in a strange context. Candidates are being prepared for a role which is at the time necessarily their own fantasy.* With other professions, some sort of practice can be possible. A trainee doctor, for example, is soon exposed to the wards. But apart from the Roman Catholic notion of deacon, most Churches do not offer genuine internships to ordinands. The powerful significance of the symbol of the priest or minister, coupled with the isolation of ministers in their daily work in churches and parishes, from the outset combine to make real practice impossible. The symbolic nature of ordination is such, for the Church, for the candidate and for the recipients of ministry, that it cannot be brought within the orbit of any pre-ordination experience.[2]

Ordinands have views on what a vicar, a priest or a minister is, does or should do. But these are illusions about themselves, because they cannot test or sense this role until they are in it. Participants in the Project, for example, commented soon after ordination, 'They never told me it would be like this.' They encountered an array of unforeseen expectations from other people, whether church members or not. Their cry was not unique; generations of their predecessors would confirm the feeling. Nevertheless, the remark exposes the problem.

(c) The Danger of Unreality

Although it may seem unduly pessimistic, we should note that the two previous points coincide in pressure to avoid any form of reality. The course or college may begin to seem like a substitute

---

* 'Fantasy' is a technical term which describes a form of imaginative activity. The content of a fantasy generally has the subject as the actor in a scene, which is to some extent distorted by defensive processes.

church. I once visited a theological college (not associated with the Project) at which a student said that he loved the worship, since it attained a degree of perfection that he 'knew' (*sic*) he would never find or be able to create in a parish. He had succumbed to the illusion that the college was the perfect church.

Lack of experience in the public role of an ordained minister may help to compound unreality. And, as has been suggested, it is possible that today's emphasis on placements may contribute, since they may themselves be idealized either as examples to be followed or instances to be avoided. Examiners in pastoral studies have reported that Anglican ordinands on the whole find theological criticism in this field bewildering. They are left with their presuppositions, which they justify as best they can with touches of sociology or psychology.

A HOLDING CONTEXT

Personal disarray, fantasy about the role of minister and the pressure to avoid reality cumulatively affect that personal and professional integration which must be central to an effective ministry. The problem, however, cannot be solved by rejigging the training; the issues are more profound, since they concern disturbance of both personal and spiritual life, which is essential in the process of a minister. A sound programme of learning for ministry requires that this fundamental disarray can be encouraged and turned to creative effect. This function is performed by a 'holding context'.*

The phrase 'holding context' derives from the technical concept of a 'holding environment'. The alteration is to dissuade any who are familiar with the original concept from applying it too rigorously in this setting. The idea of 'holding' refers to operations in dealing with people, which are both symbolic and critical in their treatment, as the following quotation makes clear:

---

* In this section some language is derived from disciplines with which theologians and educators may be unfamiliar. Generally speaking the terms have quasi-technical meanings, which are not obscure; technicalities, when used, are specifically explained.[3]

For severely *disturbed* patients, where *communication* is managed indirectly, this symbolic holding function refers to the therapist's capacity to acknowledge, bear and translate verbally into *interpretive contexts* the painful affects that are projected, induced in the therapist, or otherwise engendered through a myriad of behavioral and nonverbal means. [my italics][4]

This language may be unfamiliar but it is illuminating. We may immediately note that several themes — disturbance, communication and interpretation — are all essential in our study of ministry. To take this further, however, a brief excursus is necessary.

The concept of the holding environment was developed by D. W. Winnicott.[5] Specializing in the study and treatment of disturbed children, he discovered that the category of an autonomous individual was inappropriate. The bond between mother and child gives the child its earliest identity. Winnicott focused his attention on the mother-child bond and interpreted children's behaviour in relation to this. Like any profound insight, this sounds like a statement of the obvious. But from this perception, two key concepts about the child and its growth emerge, each of which is significant for our discussion.

The holding environment is composed from two essentials: accurate empathy and the containment of aggression. First, the child needs to be affirmed, so that she may come to some sense of herself as worthwhile and significant. She thus becomes 'good' to herself, not in a moral sense but in so far as she perceives that her mother can know her as an individual and not merely make assumptions about her. As a result she can begin to know herself, at first in relation to her mother and later in other relationships. No mother is perfect in managing this process. But she only has to be 'good enough', and so create sufficiently accurate empathy with the child for her development to take place.

The second aspect of the holding environment is the way in which aggression is contained. The growing child begins to feel and express aggressive impulses. Anyone with a small child has seen the passion which he can generate for no apparent reason. The mother's task and skill is to hold on to such aggression, thus allowing the child to learn that he does not destroy the mother or himself. Eventually these powerful emotions can be discovered to be potentially constructive. They are thus harnessed to the process of development without disrupting the relationships which are central to it.

Ordinand's are in a similar position to that of the newborn child. They need affirmation of 'goodness'. Personal disarray, coupled with uncertainty about future role, means that they need assurance about their value to God, to the Church and to the ministry. As for aggression, they are emerging from their previous self into the new creation of a neophyte minister. That process involves the channelling of struggle (a specific form of aggression) into something creative.

All education is disturbing and theological education should be intensely so. Indeed, the challenge of critical study in the setting of the exploration of an individual's spirituality is a way of deliberately creating disarray. An ordinand, therefore, must be put into an emotionally disturbing situation, where previously secure beliefs are challenged and the whole personality, or soul, is distressed. Just as the mother-child bond is given and not created, so the holding context for theological learning has to be given. In other words, it is not so much a topic for discussion as something which, because of the structure of the course, is felt as an experienced dimension of the training but something of which the participants are scarcely conscious. Without such holding there will not be a formation which will last.

The second facet of the holding environment is the containment of aggression and its transformation into positive effect. Students frequently display such aggression. It may take the form of anger expressed against someone or something outside themselves. Such aggression is easily identified as the angry person lashes out, directing this fury against someone else, whether the church authorities, tutors, people in general or God. Another possibility is that the anger can be turned upon the self. When this happens it creates apathy about one's personal life or one's role. Both sorts of behaviour are commonly observable in ministers.

THE HOLDING CONTEXT AND LEARNING FOR MINISTRY

At present, possibly because of the general uncertainty about ministry and learning for it, unifying structures are rarely apparent in courses. There is certainly no consensus about what form such a structure should take. However, using this brief discussion of the holding context, we may discern the basic requirements for which we should look in training for a contemporary and future ministry.

It needs to be coherent enough, so that the emotional and spiritual disturbance that is generated by participation and the aggression towards what is being done to the student's life and beliefs can be securely and confidently articulated. In discussion many students criticize present training on this score and the level of unfocused dissatisfaction with which ordinands arrive in their churches seems high. Courses try to meet this weakness by providing tutors or personal counsellors. But it might be better first to see that the prior need is for a resilient structure.

Since training should engender disarray, the course needs to be diverse enough to allow different viewpoints to be adopted and abandoned as the student progresses through it. The idea of a holding context is useful here. For it reminds us that any structure for enabling such developmental change must include demand as well as release. The mother, for example, does not, if she is good enough, always let the child go. Sometimes she imposes a demand against which it has to struggle.

Thirdly, the programme needs to allow students progressively to move away from its demands as they appropriate the learning. It, therefore, has to be ordered in such a way that personal and confident development of the self occurs alongside increasingly clear notions of the potential role for which the student is being trained.

In the absence of ordered thinking about structure, courses tend to become idiosyncratic. They depend for the role models, either deliberately or unconsciously, on the staff, especially the principal. The learning tends to become similarly random. Obviously many students do learn. The seriousness of the problem, however, is more specifically exposed in that they may learn in such a way that they end up with little profound and instinctive sense of two key points for contemporary ministers in the Church: first, how to interact with the culture within which the Church's ministry and mission take place; and second, how to continue a life-long process of instinctive theological reflection.

The first of these themes — the cultural environment — is the

99

specific reason for the argument that there is a rich and useful connection between such learning and the media. Before, however, that is further expounded, the other concept—that of theological reflection—must be addressed.

THEOLOGICAL REFLECTION

The phrase 'theological reflection' is widely advocated as a stance for Christian living and especially for the training and continuing education of the Churches' ministers. Yet it continues to defy definition. To those who use it and those who hear it, it sounds 'right'. But when we come to say precisely what we mean by it, we become hazy. Most of the students on the Project, for example, had heard it. But few were sure, whether for themselves or in terms of what their teachers may have had in mind, what theological reflection was.

As an all-embracing term, which describes an attitude rather than content or process, 'theological reflection' connects the four main facets of the learning process: cognitive, behavioural, affective and interpersonal.

First, there is the *cognitive* component. Learning is about thinking and developing the capacity to think, as well as about the acquisition of information and the data to use in that process. Second, there is the *behavioural* aspect. Learning is also concerned with action, what to do and how to do it. This is a particularly prominent dimension to applied theology, since without it this can drift into generalized, often anecdotal, discussion. Third we note the *affective* dimension, which is especially significant in vocational study. Feelings and how they are acknowledged and interpreted, are a core topic, which requires specific attention. Lastly, there is the *interpersonal* aspect, since learning is a collaborative activity, involving response to and with other people. At the obvious, and simplest, level there is the interaction between teacher and pupil. Today we also note the wide range of group activity in educational programmes.

These four facets to learning are, however, more than facets of learning to be incorporated into a syllabus. They also provide the dimensions of that structure by which the Churches' ministers, when they are ordained and in the public eye, will orient themselves. These men and women have to act (the behavioural facet) with sufficient distinctive learning (cognition, in this case of theology) and with a profound recognition of the importance of feelings, especially irrational ones (the affective aspect) with individuals and groups (interpersonal activity). Without integration of these four dimensions long-term effectiveness will not follow from programmes of ministerial formation.

This brings us back to theological reflection. This is both the instinctive activity of the practising minister and the heart of a structure for theological education. We may offer a working definition:

> Theological reflection is a constructed, ordered, reflective enquiry on the interaction of one's self (person and role) and one's context, which produces a conceptual framework for action.

This definition brings together much of what has been discussed earlier. The process of theological reflection is 'constructed', since without acquiring actual knowledge and the capacity to make use of it, the minister cannot embark on the process itself. This process is 'ordered', in that there are systematic approaches to such reflection. It is not a matter of lying back in a chair and 'reflecting'. The process is the more difficult one of bringing to bear on a situation or experience (which is never fully understood) such knowledge (which is always insufficient) as one can muster. Yet that situation is one in which the minister participates, or the experience is one which belongs to him or her. The process is, therefore, also 'reflective', in that the feelings generated by this experience constitute data which have to be taken into account and not ignored or discounted. And the activity as a whole is an 'enquiry', since we are always moving from the partially perceived towards what is unknown.

We now consider the focus of this enquiry. Here, as with every piece of ministry, the interest lies neither in the self alone nor in the other with whom one is dealing, whether this be another person, a group or God himself. The focal point is the interaction that is taking place between two or more parties. Theologians are accustomed to such an idea in their discussions, for example, of the doctrine of the Trinity. Here emphasis is put upon the interaction taking place between the persons or between the

Trinity and its environment. Recently similar attention has been paid to interaction as the clue to interpreting the Holy Spirit as the 'go-between' God.

Interaction is also where theological reflection occurs. One contributor to any interaction is the self. The minister examines himself, both who he is, so far as he knows (person), and what he represents (role). The concept of theological reflection at this point indicates the importance of dealing with reality. For instance, students have to examine not their potential role as ministers but their present role as learners. By doing this the stance of theological reflection becomes less a skill to be acquired than an instinctive way of responding to whatever role ministers find themselves occupying. The other part of this interaction is the context, whatever that is at any moment. Again, however, the stress is upon something specific—the immediate setting— and not on illusory notions of what this might be in the future.

Finally, the outcome of this reflection is practical, namely a course of action which is intended to bring about change in the situation which is being experienced, perceived and addressed. The primary change may come about in the minister or student (e.g. acquiring some new knowledge, which requires what was previously known to be adjusted); it may come about in the other person with whom one is dealing (e.g. effective spiritual or personal counsel); or it may be in the social behaviour of a group (e.g. a church). Whatever the action, it is always the end term in the process of theological reflection.

From this brief conspectus it will be seen that theological reflection is a realistic and practically oriented process, not an 'academic' (in its pejorative sense) stance which can be surrendered in the face of the 'genuine' demands of 'real' people.

THE MEDIA AS HOLDING CONTEXT FOR MINISTRY

We may now make the crucial connection between educational ideals and the use of the media to provide the most appropriate holding context for learning and ministry.

At a consultation on *The Cultural Power of the New Media* in 1986, James W. Carey, Dean of the College of Communications at Illinois University, was invited to respond to a day's study on the media and theological education. The participants had been mainly college teachers. He dismissed preoccupation with technique and technology: 'You can learn to write or to do a TV program in six months. Only to speak is hard.' He then continued:

> I spend all my time trying to rejuvenate the effects of the liberal arts. I say, 'Why aren't you teaching politics? History? English?' But everyone's interested in 'media'—the simple subject—not the important, complex subjects.[6]

Carey's remarks are valuable. Few would dissent from his view that technology and technique are not immediately important for theological education or ministry. But there is also a danger that to focus on the media in any way might be an avoidance of the harder matters of learning and the capacity to speak—that is, having something to say.

In our extended argument about theological education, however, the 'complex subjects' of content of learning, process of reflection and the accompanying emotional disturbance have been central. Indeed, it is because of these subjects that a basic requirement for a programme of contemporary theological education is a holding context. The proposal now is that, far from being one component (however seductive by comparison with the older disciplines) in theological education, the media best provide exactly such holding. This would also seem to be the case for the foreseeable future. For the media as a phenomenon constitute the primary cultural context for contemporary life. So the proposal is not for a temporary shift in the approach to such education; it implies a long-term adjustment.

This proposal does not imply that the customary contents and disciplines of theological study should be abandoned in favour of media studies. Bible, doctrine, pastoral studies, liturgy, etc. all retain their place in the curriculum. Nor is it suggested that courses should be converted into programmes of communications' studies, although one outcome might be that students would explore more fully the nature of appropriate forms of discourse (what Carey called 'the difficulty of speaking') and the variety of contexts within which the gospel is today to be communicated. It is the pervasive presence and impact of the media in our culture that suggests that they provide an excellent basis for that holding context which vocational training needs. A number of preliminary points may be made; in Part III we shall turn to details.

First, the media, notably television, now draw people's attention to the global culture in which they participate. This may lead to the loss of a clear sense of place in the world, from which one outcome may be a relativistic attitude. But the process may also be enlarging. People now have more knowledge about themselves and their world than their predecessors had. Attention to the media, therefore, brings to the fore the complex personal, local and universal frames within which the Church now exists and has to interpret its gospel. To take the media as the basis for a holding context is, as education in general should be, potentially to enlarge one's horizons without succumbing to despair at their vastness. One outcome is a higher self-esteem and consequently valuing of others.

A further effect of such revaluing may be discerned when we see that the media may be directing attention to necessary changes in theology itself. They may, for instance, help to explain some of the current movements in theological thinking by placing them in the global culture. This is not to suggest that there will not be straightforward programmes of exposition of the theological undergirding that the Western Christian tradition provides for the Churches' life. But the range of information provided through the media allows students to earth in a specific social background what they discover about theological endeavour in different parts of the world. In terms of academic rigour and precision this may seem a sketchy way to proceed. But when we recall that we are primarily concerned with vocational learning, which demands a practical or applied outcome, then such niceties are less important.

The next point frequently emerged during the work of the Project and has already been mentioned in passing. When the scope of the individual's knowledge and information is greatly enlarged, a natural response is to turn back to the known (oneself) and become inwardly reflective. Because the world appears so vast, the self takes on new prominence.

In courses the response may be institutionalized. These may emphasize the personal growth of each student and the fellowship of the whole at the expense of content and of the stress of learning. The idea of the holding context, however, is designed to enable both these aspects, individual value and contained aggression (in this case against learning itself), to be handled. Taking the media, therefore, as the means to conceptualize the holding context of theological education will usefully encourage attention to that question of personal spirituality and affirmation that we earlier noted as one of the integrating aspects of theological education.

Thirdly, and most importantly, the media provide the student with a notional, but at the same time examinable, role against which they may test all their learning—cognitive, behavioural, affective and interpersonal. The key term here is 'role'. We have frequently commented that the public role of the minister is not available to the ordinand as a referent during training. At this stage it is a fantasy. To use it, therefore, as if it were genuine, encourages fantasies about the Church and the minister, which may be profitably shaken up when the minister starts work. But equally this may not happen, with consequently detrimental effects on the minister, his ministry and the Church.

The precise role which will be assigned to the student in this media constructed holding, is that of 'communicator'. This role requires students to be aware that they are participants in a media-saturated society. This is the first stage of becoming consciously inculturated: to be aware of who I am, not just as a person but as citizen, student or minister.[7]

Additionally such an approach encourages the recognition of other dimensions to modern life. For example, it becomes apparent that the Church is not the sole bearer of ritual in a secular world. Indeed, the media may even be regarded as a form of surrogate religion. But examination of this issue takes students not just to the media but through them to the whole area of religion itself. Comparisons between the media as the conveyors of contemporary culture and the Church as the transmitter of a culture—whether in conflict or not is part of the argument—brings the reality of the contemporary Church to the fore.

These are preliminary indicators of what will follow. But we can begin to see how the media, as holding context, press home reality, both to the notion of role with which students and ministers operate, and to the Church or institution which authorizes and will authorize them.

Notes

1. Jürgen Moltmann, *The Crucified God* (London, SCM, 1973), pp. 7–32.

2. There are serious behavioural and dynamic reasons why this is so, which are frequently overlooked in plans for ministerial training. See, for example, Bruce Reed, *The Dynamics of Religion*: Wesley Carr, *The Priestlike Task*; also 'Working with Dependency and Remaining Sane', in Giles Ecclestone, ed., *The Parish Church?* (London, Mowbray, 1988), pp. 99ff.

3. For an example of specific application of such thinking to adult education, see John Hull, *What Prevents Adult Christians from Learning* (London, SCM, 1985).

4. Edward Shapiro and Wesley Carr, 'Disguised Countertransference in Institutions', *Psychiatry* 50 (1987), p. 73.

5. D. W. Winnicott, 'The Theory of the Parent–Infant Relationship', *International Journal of Psycho-Analysis* 41 (1960), pp. 585ff. See also for more recent discussion of the general importance of this concept, A. Modell, *Psychoanalysis in a New Context* (New York, International Universities Press, 1985).

6. *Cultural Power of the New Media*, p. 15.

7. This idea of the cultural earthing of theological education is familiar with reference to the Third World. See, for example, Christine Lienemann-Perrin, *Training for Relevant Ministry: A Study of the Work of the Theological Education Fund* (Madras, The Christian Literature Society, 1981).

Part Three

INTRODUCTION

How are the theories in the previous four chapters to be put into practice? This final section is about that question. At first sight it may seem interesting only to theological educators. This is not, however, the intention. The content, method and process for the programme which is sketched here is only a specific example of how discipleship and learning may come about in our media-saturated age. With a few adjustments these suggestions apply equally to a diocesan training programme or the endeavours of a local congregation. They also indicate some of the larger theological questions which are raised by attention to the media.

What follows is an example. Anything more would be presumptuous and foolhardy, since too many issues are not discussed. For example, models of learning are essential. So this emphatically is not a blue-print. It claims to be no more than an indication of what attention to theological education might produce, when the discussion of culture and the media which has preceded is taken seriously.

> I find myself gradually reorientating myself from the highly academic approach of theological college to one which is more experiential, multi-disciplinary and less speculative. It is good to have the theology under my belt in order — hopefully — to be discerning about religious questions, but I find it increasingly difficult to couch my world view in solely Christian terms.

This statement was made by one of the students on the Project during his first year as an ordained minister. He had not felt his training was deficient. Nor was he anti-academic; indeed he had a distinguished record of learning and, more than some of his colleagues, spoke favourably about the training which he had been offered at his theological college. But, probably without his realizing it, he was passing an acute judgement on that training, not least with the words 'experiential, multi-disciplinary and less speculative'.

The experience of new ministers is likely to press them towards a more experiential approach to theological thinking, as they bring their learning into contact with people's everyday life. We have previously noted this issue as the problem of finding a genuine context within which to set theological education. 'Multi-disciplinary' implies that the speaker sought a more profound integration of disciplines in himself as he began to minister to people in their complexity. This, too, we have discussed. 'Less speculative' is especially intriguing. For this young minister seemed to be finding that his difficulty in creating a theologically sound practice of ministry required from him a distinctive development in style and content of theological thinking. It was not a matter of leaving behind what had been learned or discovering that his training had, in any pejorative sense, been 'too academic'. Something new was required: not an application of old learning but the creation of a new style of reflection and action.

Learning for ministry, before and after ordination, is an applied enterprise, which needs to be as consonant as possible in its style with the experience that awaits the minister.

> To reflect theologically on the practice of ministry is to be engaged in a cyclical process of integration, disintegration, under pressure from the realities of ministry or of fresh theological insights, and subsequent reintegration.[1]

The test of any proposals about training is whether they commend themselves to professionals in the field and whether they work. In the case of a book like this, the reader's question is perhaps simpler: How would things be affected in practice, if I took the media into account as proposed? The Project eventually aims to produce curriculum proposals. As will by now be clear, these need to be more radical than merely drafting courses in communication, exploring (as best we may) the effects of the media, examining religious television, and the like. Equally becoming accustomed to using the modern technology of the media — video cameras, video pictures, even interactive video, in addition to the old stand-by of hands-on studio practice — does not mean that the context of the media has been taken into account. The question is deeper and more problematic.

Nevertheless, however difficult the question, the question of how the present discussion has an impact on theological education must be answered. Part III, therefore, consists of an argument for an approach to theological education which takes seriously the media-saturated context of contemporary life.

Four topics are taken as the foundations of the enterprise of theological education: preaching, pastoring, spiritual formation and leadership/social skills. They have not been arbitrarily selected. They were identified by the participants in the Project, both when, as students, they reflected on their training and when, as neophyte ministers, they began to find what demands were made upon them. These themes, therefore, are the main areas of applied theological learning which the Church and its ministers seem to require. On the other hand, in some form or other these four topics have traditionally formed the basis of theological education.

Each of them, however familiar it may appear, is now modified from two perspectives: first, 'the broadcasting input'—the impact of the cultural phenomenon of the media on the process and content of theological learning; and second, the consequences for this area of life and Christian ministry of working in a media-saturated world. The various aspects of the process of theological reflection, which was discussed in theoretical and general terms above, now become specific.

For convenience a schematic outline of the programme will be found on page 114.

Note

1. John Foskett and David Lyall, *Helping the Helpers: Supervision and Pastoral Care* (London, SPCK, 1988), p. 47.

8 THE MEDIA AND LEARNING
FOR MINISTRY

The media have been proposed as a holding context for the attempt at formation which can produce integrated ministers in the confusing context of today's world. There remains, however, the matter of content. Unexpectedly the style of the mass media also illuminates this. According to a classic definition they should inform, entertain and educate. But in practice these three aspects are inseparable. There is an overarching task of gaining and holding an audience, which appears with varying emphases in different settings. For instance, even the most banal game-show notionally offers viewers and participants some opportunities for learning. And intellectually stimulating programmes must entertain. The tensions between the three aims become acute in presentation of the news. Our present discussion, however, is illuminated, if we recognize that learning cannot be pursued without information, and information (content) cannot be considered without our paying attention to entertainment (that is, presentation and process).

MEDIA, CONTENT AND STYLE IN THEOLOGICAL EDUCATION

Learning for ministry needs to escape the restrictive tyranny of the styles of teaching which are associated with traditional disciplines, without inadvertently discarding or devaluing those disciplines themselves. In recent years efforts have been made to integrate the content of the different subjects with the wider demands of vocational education. But to many it now seems increasingly probable that this aim, worthy as it is, cannot in fact be achieved. However careful the attempt, two outcomes ensue: either one subject is implicitly devalued and the familiar academic competition for significance emerges; or the subtle ordering of a structured curriculum remains beyond the comprehension of the students, who become increasingly confused in their learning and disaffected.

The study of the Old Testament, a subject which many consider important, illustrates this dilemma. It might be thought that the intensive examination of these texts over the past two centuries should have produced 'assured conclusions'. That assumption, however, is delusive. Indeed the Old Testament increasingly presents problems to students, ministers and experts alike.

Proposals for training, therefore, must co-ordinate continuing problems of content, style and process in a way similar to that in which the media have to balance information, education and entertainment. When the media are taken seriously, they illuminate this problem.

But there is a further reason for looking to the media. Any teaching programme which is based on this approach will inevitably be aligned with the main cultural style prevailing within our society. The connections, therefore, between theology and people's lives, or between the process of theological education and the context of ministry (the issue of 'relevance') will become more prominent and points which ministers instinctively grasp.

EDUCATING MEDIA-AWARE MINISTERS

Four main areas of study can now be identified, together with three essential stances which should influence each of them. This scheme (see p. 114), like all such diagrams, is oversimplified. The first four columns represent the main components in any programme of theological education. Underneath each is a brief description of the task of ministry which it aims to cover. Below this are listed, first, the chief disciplines that are pertinent to it, followed by specific fields of imaginative learning and the particular applied skill that it demands. Obviously there is no absolute division between each topic: they, too, will interact. It is, for example, important to note how 'liturgy' appears in each of them in different guises.

On the right hand side there is a fifth column labelled 'Media'. Underneath are the three terms which influence the whole enterprise. These fields arise from consideration of the media and of communications studies: broadcasting, literary/art studies, and communication theory. It is not suggested that

113

PREACHING	PASTORING	SPIRITUAL FORMATION	LEADERSHIP AND SOCIAL SKILLS	MEDIA
Aimed at, but not exclusively for, the congregation, i.e. discipleship	Aimed at all people, whatever their formal connection with the Church, i.e. mission	Aimed at the minister's self, i.e. growth in person & role	Aimed at the church as a unit, i.e. collaboration	
COMMUNICATING Interpreting the tradition: Bible Doctrine Philosophy History	CONTEMPORARY STORIES Internalized gospel for use: Sociology Psychology Ethics	MEANINGS Living publicly what is prayed: Practice of prayer Integrating learning and life	MODELS Joining oneself to others: models of church styles of leadership	BROADCASTING
GENRES Communication and hermeneutic Liturgy & Symbols Sacraments	PEOPLE (Novels) Media as assumptive world Liturgy	POETRY AND ART Images Iconography Imagining		LITERARY/ARTS STUDIES
SKILLS	HUMAN INTERACTIONS	COMMUNICATION WITH THE OTHER	TASKS AND ROLES	COMMUNICATION THEORY

these studies should be intruded into or allowed to dominate the mainline disciplines of theological education which are listed as the four main heads. They constitute the basic informative approaches which run through all this learning. Schematically they represent the practical outworking of the concept of the media as the holding context for theological education.

So, for example, 'Broadcasting', which (particularly as television) is the dominant medium, operates in PREACHING to remind teacher and student alike of the variety of communication which those addressed, as well as the preacher/teacher, experience; in PASTORING it may provide stories from which learning may follow; in SPIRITUAL FORMATION it supplies instances of meaning, questions about this being raised even among the most trivial productions; and in LEADERSHIP AND SOCIAL SKILLS it offers a series of viewable models.

Likewise 'Literary/arts studies' suggest GENRES for the hermeneutical task; accessible psychological and sociological insights into PEOPLE and their behaviour; and imaginative iconography, POETRY AND ART, for the spiritual life. They essentially perform a mind-enlarging function.

'Communication theory' introduces learning about SKILLS; techniques for thinking about HUMAN INTERACTION; profound questions about the nature of spiritual behaviour, COMMUNICATING WITH THE OTHER, whether this be God or one's neighbour; and clarity about TASK AND ROLE in leadership.

One participant in the Project commented on his experience of his first Christmas in the parish:

> College had little to offer by way of helping prepare us for ministering to the many who only attend church for the major festivals or come only to see their child perform in a play. Yet as a mission-field the Christmas run-up is unparalleled, if the Church can take hold of it.

This is a common experience among ministers, but in the light of this draft curriculum it is especially interesting. For in this statement the speaker succinctly includes the problems of pastoring (mission); the question of genre in preaching (communicating the gospel); his own discomfort at not knowing how to evaluate what was happening (lack of spiritual formation); and finally the organizational question — 'If the Church can take hold of it'.

115

CONCLUSION

There is no suggestion here that, if the proposals outlined in this book are adopted, a minister's life will become simpler. Hopefully, however, we should be working towards a Church for today which, not least through its ministers and leaders, can do a number of things better: interpret the gospel more appopriately in various situations with more confidence; train its ministers and members to grasp what is happening to the gospel in this media-saturated environment; develop a life which is more at one with those among whom it tries to minister and which is organizing itself more simply and more effectively for its tasks.

9 PREACHING

Whatever the arguments about ministry and the role of ministers, all agree that a minister must be someone instructed in the Scriptures and the Christian tradition. The ideal of the minister as a learned person has become less prominent in recent decades. But the educational function remains. Ministers are expected to be able to instruct the people of God, both young people and adults. Even when they possess no specifically educational skills, they are required to preach. This is an historic expectation in the Free Church and Anglican traditions, and since Vatican II has also become more prominent in the Roman Catholic Church.

In this chapter the whole educational function of the minister is subsumed under the heading 'Preaching'. *Kerygma* (proclamation) is inherent in the Christian gospel. All that is known or believed has an inbuilt dimension of communication. The minister as educator or preacher presents the gospel as a way of discipleship, which is to be studied, learned and lived.

BROADCASTING AND PREACHING

Broadcasting impacts on this aspect of the syllabus chiefly in two areas: the study of communication in itself, and consideration of the media-saturated environment as the contemporary context for the word. Communications' theory is specifically studied at this point in the syllabus. On the whole it has been neglected in the study of theology. Edmund Leach, for instance, in a discussion of the logic of sacrifice, has noted how extensively this theme has been explored in theological literature with scarcely any reference to anthropology. In fact this judgement is inaccurate when we think of Old Testament research. But it is generally true that such integrating links across the Testaments into Christian doctrine are missing from many programmes.[1]

Since the chief area of interpretation is the tradition and data needs to be acquired, the content looks unoriginal — Bible, Doctrine and History. The more important question, however, is what style of study will be congruent with the integration of learning and ministry which is demanded in a media-saturated society.

The underlying question to be addressed to any author, ancient or modern, is the communications' question. This best takes the shape of Leonard Hodgson's famous dictum, which is variously reported but roughly was: 'What must the truth be now, if people who thought as the biblical writers did put it like that?'[2] Hodgson was talking about a stance rather than suggesting that there is a body of truth which has merely to be expressed in different language in each new generation. Indeed, even if that were once thought, contemporary communications' theory undermines any such facile belief.

This approach, for instance, would enliven examination of the concept of 'word'. This could be tested by reference to different media. In the USA, for example, Churches have had to examine the tele-evangelists and the concept of gospel which emerges in their message and behaviour. Dismissing this as an excrescence on the fringe of American religious life cannot suffice. The phenomenon may prove ephemeral. But the question which this use of television poses to the Churches and especially ministers concerns the nature of their own pastoral and preaching behaviour and the assumptions upon which that is based. A sociological 'explanation' is not enough. There is a dogmatic issue to be faced: What aspect of the Christian gospel leads to this phenomenon? What are the deficiencies in the message which we are proclaiming that produce such compensation? And, as a point of historical and theological study, where else in the history of Scripture and of the Church's tradition does any interface between a theological inheritance and a new human demand produce a significant development in the gospel? And how do we test (and how have our predecessors tested) such changes for legitimacy? In the course of Christian history such interaction occurs between inherited belief and new knowledge, until the crucial transition of the Enlightenment is reached and its consequences pursued. Each of these encounters becomes something about which data are required: traditional learning, and *at the same time*, a paradigm for the minister's own activity.

We should not, however, think that these courses are simply

the old ones with the word 'communications' added. This dimension brings critical additions to thinking about the content of theology, as well as questions of religious communication.

The first is obvious, but in the wordy atmosphere of theological study may be overlooked—the primary referent in religion, 'God', is inexpressible. There is always the question of translation. We might, for instance, take up from a communications' perspective how Paul interprets the story of Jesus for the different world of Asia Minor. Issues of faithfulness and novelty become central and these are one aspect of communication. Narrative theology might inform such study.

But behind this familiar theological problem lies the more fundamental question of knowledge of God. How can something which is apprehended by so strange a means as faith be communicated at all? A philosophical concern thus emerges and philosophy is needed at the heart of biblical and historical study. It is not a prolegomenon or optional discipline. Thus integration through communications begins and the same questions are addressed to the Bible class as to the philosophy of religion group.

This point goes to the heart of ministerial formation. The Roman Catholic Church has recently noted that the large amount of learning which it required of its seminarians may have obscured the task of helping the student to *be* a priest.[3] Training in other Churches may have become preoccupied with the person of the candidate and diminished the emphasis upon knowledge and learning. These educational arguments are not easily resolved. All, however, agree that who the minister is conveys at least as much of the gospel as what he teaches. By taking seriously the communications' facet to the study of traditional disciplines we can relate these studies to the formation of the minister. The notion of 'being' is essentially to do with communicating. Ministers do not exist in isolation; they are bearers of the gospel and so, we may say, through their lives they communicate it. Here belief, what has been believed and what is believed, is integrated in the person of the believing student. Historical transitions and new translations of the gospel can be examined and the continuing effect on the present day Church and its future ministers explored in an integrated fashion.

LITERARY/ARTS STUDIES AND PREACHING

At this point the idea of 'interpretation' reappears. If the phenomenon of the mass media informs the study of doctrine, Bible and history by drawing attention to the history and dynamic of human communication, the question of interpretation arises through literary studies. The contemporary hermeneutic of Scripture is closely related to literary study and so fits naturally here. The issue of communication inevitably draws attention to its complexity and hence to the distinctive activity of theological learning. There is a general problem of hermeneutics, which would apply to the use of any text, ancient or modern. But seeing Scripture as part of the context within which communication is being attempted draws the student's attention to the specific characteristics of the books of the Bible and to the issues which are raised when we claim status for them as in some sense the Word of God.[4]

The question of genre, however, also introduces a major topic for religious communication—symbolism. In most Churches today the twinning of word and sacrament has become commonplace. The proclamation of the gospel is perceived as something more than words. There is an affective interchange, for example, which a symbol makes possible in a way that a sermon does not. We shall return to this in more detail when thinking about spiritual formation. For the moment, however, we note that there is a missionary aspect to the Church's symbolism.

> Christianity is not only a structure of the intellect, it is also a structure of experience through which *felt* knowledge that eludes any dragooning by words fires the imagination and generates visionary energy. . . . the importance *of* the Church as a symbol in the Television Age will grow . . . The Church is a public symbol that challenges the privatisation of life; a symbol of assembly which works against isolation and fragmentation; a symbol of corporate action at a time of individual passivity . . . A resurgence of image-making ought not to be beyond a Church whose Lord mediated himself through a multitude of things that captivated the senses—bread, water, sweat, silver, gold, a couple of crossed lines, blood, white, a cry, lover, fish, vinegar, purple.[5]

This passage reads optimistically but makes an essential point: study of the basic information, which is rightly expected of any minister, needs to be set not only in terms of the communications' questions that are raised by it but also of the range of communication in which a symbolic body like the Church participates. Sacramental theology, therefore, does not merely emerge as study of the sacraments but moves towards that range of human studies to which Leach drew attention. For in the realm of symbol, especially natural symbols, the Church finds that it has no ownership, even of its apparently most distinctive possessions, bread, wine, water and light.

Two further issues are also illuminated by assigning the media-saturated world prominence in reflection on this aspect of ministry: one is that of integrity, with the concomitant risk of seduction; the other is the increasingly significant issue of religious pluralism.

Entertainment, information and education are not discrete aspects of the media but are inextricably intertwined. Great preachers have instinctively held these three facets of communication together. In the age before the mass media there is little doubt that men like Wesley, Whitfield, Spurgeon and Moody (and, in the twilight of that era, Weatherhead, Sangster, Lloyd-Jones, and Stott) were entertainers. Their integrity, however, was unquestioned. Today, however, the seduction of entertainment has become more serious and every presentation of the gospel needs examining for the connection of its style to the nature of belief.

Postman tells the story of a rabbi who proposed to engage Luciano Pavarotti to sing the prayer *Kol Nidre* in his synagogue at the beginning of Yom Kippur. 'He believes that the event would fill the synagogue as never before. Who can doubt it? But as Hannah Arendt would say, *that* is the problem, not a solution to one.'[6] The seduction of entertainment, not least in the field of the public preacher (as witnessed also by the electronic churches in the USA) is not in doubt. The preaching component in ministerial formation needs also to be deliberately counter-cultural.

We have noted the capacity of a dominant mass medium, such as television, not only to ensnare people's minds but also to arouse and sustain significant dissent. Audiences are not as passive as was at one time believed. There is, therefore, in this both a warning to the Christian communicator and an encouragement. The warning is the danger of being seduced into a simplistic view of communication; the encouragement is in the continuing capacity of people to engage with ideas.

There is, incidentally, a further point which is relevant here. Religion, even in the increasingly secularized West, is supposed to be to some degree socially subversive. Maintenance of the Church is frequently contrasted with its mission. Prospectuses advertise that the course is designed to free students (and hence ministers) so that they can lead the Churches to become more radical than they are at present. But the fact remains that the Churches as we know them, rather than as we might like them to be, are the given material with which ministers have to work. Longing glances at, for example, liberation theology may not facilitate theological and pastoral enterprise in Western Europe. But with careful attention to the nature of the media in our culture, it would be possible to explore the subversive (or converting) power of the gospel in the light of realism.

The second issue presented is contemporary religious pluralism, which is a crucial context for today's ministry. Using media presentations explicitly, and their seductions within the Christian field, can be a way of bringing home the variety of religious options before people today. This study will include those aspects of the self that are attracted and repelled by the various strands of religious activity and the consequent responses, as well as the social issues that this factor indicates.

Commenting on the story of the rabbi and Pavarotti, Postman says: 'Christianity is a demanding and serious religion. When it is delivered as easy and amusing, it is *another kind of religion altogether*' (my italics). When we realize that Christianity may not merely take various forms but can sometimes appear to transform itself into something quite different from what we expect — another religion — we are carried simultaneously into the realm of religious pluralism and our own religious confession. Pluralism is not a matter of the variety of faiths which may be studied. It is about the increased range of possible beliefs even within one faith such as Christianity. Such a variety is no longer confined to the main church divisions but is to be found within each Church and each believer. For every minister there is, therefore, an essential task of exploring such attitudes, beliefs and responses.

COMMUNICATION THEORY AND PREACHING

One further point remains in considering preaching in the light of the media. Coherence between the subject being studied and the method of study is essential. This is a basic insight from communications' studies and from reflections on the media themselves. In other words, in the preaching perspective teacher and students must interact in a style which is congruent with the subject. The lecture, for example, has known limitations as a method of teaching. A graffito at King's College, London, read: 'Definition of a lecture: a means of transferring the notes of the lecturer to the notes of his audience without it passing through the minds of either.' But this sort of comment will not be the ground on which a particular method of teaching will be questioned. In view of the emphasis upon communication as interactive, the teaching and learning style will have to be similarly designed.

In some contemporary educational theory, for example, the use of the small group becomes the model. When, therefore, this is the medium, the implicit message needs examining. This study directs us to the historical and theological questions about the nature of the Church. Is it, for instance, ideally thought of in terms of small groups? If such an assumption is made, what are the consequences not only for the life of the congregation but also for our theological reflection on the way that God interacts communicatively with men and women? The applied pastoral questions of theology become immediate. And the historical, literary issue will not be far away. For example, is the Sermon on the Mount a sermon addressed by a speaker to an audience, an interactive seminar or a small group exercise?

Here, too, the matter of acquiring communications' skills becomes prominent. These have so far been steadily set to one side, but they cannot and should not be ignored. How to capture people's attention; how to structure an address that will carry them to a new perception of God and the gospel; how to cope with altered time spans of concentration; how and when to illustrate—these and similar questions of technique are faced at this point.

Much can be learned from professional communicators in the media. Yet experience often proves these to be the very people who are least competent at teaching. The reason lies in a central point in communications' studies: there are styles of communication which are suitable to certain settings and material. Thus while learning a few useful techniques, the student will also be pushed back to the underlying theological and philosophical problems of preaching which cannot be surmounted by skills alone.

Some people may reckon that preaching should not be assigned so high a profile in the training of the next generation of the Churches' ministers. There is a discernible undercurrent of dissaffection with this familiar church activity. Whatever the case, however, preaching is not being here proposed as a single activity but as a focal point around which, when we free it from the traditional view of the preacher, the pulpit and the congregation, many aspects of practical ministry coalesce.

Notes

1. Leach, *Culture and Communication*, pp. 81ff.

2. Leonard Hodgson, *For Faith and Freedom* (London, Darton, Longman & Todd, 2nd edn, 1968), p. x.

3. The [RC] Bishops' Conference of England and Wales, *Ministry and Mission: Proposals for a National Policy for Lifelong Priestly Formation. Briefing* 17 (1987), pp. 218ff.

4. Anthony Thiselton, *The Two Horizons* (Exeter, Paternoster, 1980).

5. Colin Morris, *God in a Box* (London, Hodder & Stoughton, 1984), pp. 204ff.

6. Postman, *Amusing Ourselves to Death*, p. 126.

10 PASTORING

The term 'pastor' is notoriously wide-ranging and difficult to define. The model of shepherd and sheep has become inadequate. This is not solely because that sort of simple relationship is increasingly foreign to the contemporary world. The Churches' ministries over the centuries have had their effect. For whereas the shepherd with his flock may describe a small, gathered church with its pastor, few such churches now exist. Most ministers in the mainstream Churches find that their activity is not confined to those who enrol as church members or with those who worship and who affirm the Christian faith. They also encounter many who may claim to belong: 'This has always been our church'; 'We're Catholic', but who rarely, if ever, come to the church. Whatever their faith, it is nearer half-belief than total commitment.

One essential of sensitive pastoral ministry is the ability to perceive the story in which the pastor is being involved. He or she is not just being told something: people speak in a context which is created by their interaction with the minister as representative of something. Within a congregation there may be certain accepted stories, as, for example, those in Scripture or those from the history of the local church's life. The pastor will often use these to discover the precise context of a particular encounter. But the wider range of pastorings also needs consciously to be held in mind. The pastor, therefore, is here first regarded as essentially a missionary.

Pastoring is more wide-ranging than it is often thought to be. It is not limited to pastoral counselling or care. In this outline the word refers to the total stance of the Church *ad extra*. It, therefore specifically includes that part of the minister's activity where expectations are focused from outside the Church more than from within its membership. We are discussing all activities of the Church with those among whom it is set — mission.

A common complaint about ministers and their present training is that they are not prepared for mission. Such remarks probably indicate the way in which uncomfortable aspects of Christian commitment are most conveniently focused in authorized leaders. Those who look to their ministers to be missionary leaders are unlikely to have any more idea what this means than they have. One point, however, is indisputable: today's Churches and ministers must study how they engage with people around the fringes of the Church and beyond. It is also clear that ministers must be able to acquire ways of interpreting this engagement, especially by learning how to think of people, their presuppositions and the context within which they live. Recently there has been a trend towards offering ministers some psychological and sociological insights. But attention to the media raises important questions about this assumption.

BROADCASTING AND PASTORING

From the previous discussion about the media as context, it is clear that learning about pastoring will be the component of the syllabus which will make the most straightforward use of media material. Consideration of the media and communications inevitably increases ministers' awareness of other people, especially those with whose life-style and attitudes they are themselves unfamiliar. This in itself is the major step in the practice of mission.

The mass media have enormous input to people's lives since they generate and distribute contemporary stories. The influence of soap operas is one instance. But advertisements, too, generate stories, about how life ought to be and how it could be. Some of these become serialized 'stories': we are enticed into the lives of others, where the product is a symbol of status or affection and, as we await the next twist in the saga, we buy the product. It is as if advertisers have rediscovered that human beings are entranced by stories. Considering these myth factories we may be reminded of James Curran's remarks in which he contrasted the role of the modern mass media with that of the medieval Church.[1] Each in their way knew that people need stories and that effective communication of ideas is through narrative and illustration.

To live confidently in the worlds of people's own stories — their descriptions of their lives (or, at least, parts of them) into which they may invite the minister — pastors need so to have internalized their own story and the gospel that it can be explored by others in them.[2] One way to do that is to become aware of the way in which stories develop and are used. We shall turn below to the significance of literary studies. Another avenue to such learning lies through the study of sociology and psychology.

We may now amplify the earlier comment on the place of these disciplines in the minister's learning. Introductory work in these fields is often regarded as marginal. There is good reason for this. Bits of social science, often offered through occasional seminars and one-off lectures, are too sketchy to be useful and too isolated to be integrated so that their contribution becomes self-evident.

The sociological and psychological study of religion tends paradoxically to appear either too generalized or too specific. On the one hand, theories may be interesting, but seem remote from the students' present experience of the Church or of themselves. On the other hand, case studies are easily dismissed as particular instances and, by inference, as special pleading. Ministers claim uniqueness for their Churches and their experience as a defence against having to examine their ministry by comparing it with that of others.

Once again, therefore, we come up against a major problem in learning for ministry: what constitutes an agreed context? Here the media become explicitly important. For rather than studying particular Churches, with the limitations to such learning, ministers may, through attention to the media, study the society of which their Churches are part and in which their ministry is exercised. What is more, their own experience as viewers or listeners is an integral component of the study. Far from being dismissed as irrelevant, such study and learning will always have significance.[3]

From the schematic presentation on p. 114 it will be noted that the study of ethics is included in this section. Ministers often comment that they are more in demand for ethical advice and pastoral guidance than for 'straightforward' theological teaching. Yet it has from time to time proved difficult to know where to locate the study of ethics in courses of theological education. In a pluralist world and its corollary, ecumenically reflective Churches, we should not be surprised at such uncertainty. Since, however, ethical study has its practical outcome for the minister in moral decisions (or, at least, advice about them), a programme in applied theology will place ethical study close to other thinking about the interaction of the Church and its ministers with those outside or on the fringe. This stance is consonant with today's acknowledgement of the significance of social determinants in ethical thinking.[4] By regarding pastors and those among whom they minister as 'media-saturated', we have an integrating point around which to earth sociological, psychological and ethical learning. For whatever else the media do, their productions starkly expose ethical dilemmas.

LITERARY/ARTS STUDIES AND PASTORING

Turning to the input of Literary/Arts Studies, we face a most important facet of learning for pastoring. Novels are essential ingredients in such training. We have noted that the term 'media' refers to more than the mass media. Novels emphasize the importance of stories, their telling and hearing. In particular they possess one dimension which the other media lack—space. Not only is there greater spaciousness in the telling of stories on pages; the experience of readers is also different from that of viewers or listeners: they have greater control. A book can be laid down and taken up again at will. The story, therefore, can be 'heard' in a more leisurely fashion.

This observation connects with that of the place of sociology and psychology in theological education. The importance of these subjects is indisputable, but it is possible, when they are not made the core topic of a syllabus, to approach them tangentially. A great deal can be learned through the various media, not least from reading modern literature and novels. To the objection that in our society reading novels is an élitist activity, the riposte is that the reflective insights into human behaviour that a novelist offers are a means of making the minister more alert to the complexity and privilege of his pastoring task. In other words, the sociological and psychological awareness that a minister will find stimulating to theological reflection may be acquired through media-related teaching of these subjects.

So far we have taken 'pastoring' in a general sense. Within that, however, there is the specific function of the pastor. This role is not the same as that of the pastoral counsellor, but subject to that proviso the following comment is apposite to thinking about a curriculum for theological education:

> The pastoral counsellor is not only a listener to stories; he or she is also the bearer of stories and a story. The pastoral counsellor does not come empty handed to the task of understanding the other's story and offering the possibility of a new interpretation. The pastoral counsellor brings his or her own interpretation of life experience with its use of both commonly held symbols, images and themes from the cultural milieu of the counsellor and the private, nuanced meanings that have been shaped by the pastoral counsellor's own life experience and its private interpretation.[5]

This quotation is a valuable reminder of the nature of the minister's roles in dealing with people, both individuals and groups, especially those outside the gathered congregation. Ministers are the bearers of a story—not, as may sometimes be assumed, the 'simple gospel' story of Jesus, but the more complex story which is generated by what they are believed to stand for, what they themselves believe, and what is created by those interactions in a specific situation. Indeed it is in such encounters that gospel is both discerned and created and the familiar media notion of the intertwining of content and process finds its theological correspondence. Pastoring is a form of hermeneutical activity.[6]

A significant form of such activity occurs in rites and their accompanying rituals. Here, too, attention to the media as a cultural phenomenon enables learning to be earthed. Theological students are not yet themselves symbolic figures. As a result, their learning about ritual may tend to be either cerebral or confined to the niceties of ecclesiastical behaviour. This can be particularly true of teaching on liturgy. The cultural dimension of the media, however, comprises a ritual common language, which is shared alike by teacher, student and others. The universalizing pressure of the media can become the basis of learning about the missionary and pastoral aspect of the Church's particular rituals, both the formal and the informal. For at the very least it can remind all concerned of the potency of what they are being invited to handle.

> Cultural phenomena, especially of a symbolic and mythic kind, are curiously resistant to being imprisoned in one unequivocal 'meaning'. They constantly escape from the boxes into which rational analysis tries to pack them: they have a Protean quality which seems to evade definitive translation into non-symbolic—that is, cold, unresonant, totally explicit, once-for-all accurate terms ... The disciplines of literary, music and art criticism are after all premised on the inexhaustibility of meaning and relevance in the cultural artifacts which form their subject matter.[7]

An instinctive grasp of this central factor in ministry requires practice. Yet since such experience cannot be acquired until the public role of minister has been taken up and can therefore be responded to by others, there remains a persistent dilemma at the heart of theological education. A useful approach to this problem, however, is offered by a more extensive use of the media in courses. These are major carriers of contemporary stories. There is no escaping this, even by those who believe that they remain unaffected by not owning a television set, by selectively listening to the radio, or by not reading newspapers. By considering excerpts from media productions, it is possible to increase ministers' awareness of stories (both in the verbal and ritual sense) and their potency.

COMMUNICATION THEORY AND PASTORING

The specific skills that the minister might expect to acquire in this part of the course are to do with interactions between individuals and groups. The emphasis upon media and communications especially clarifies one disputed area of the Churches' dealings with people. A perennial debate on evangelism and mission concerns the difference between proclamation and propaganda. The former is required of Christians; and latter is inappropriate to the gospel. In the light of the media and communications' theory, proclamation may be seen as essentially interactive. Proclaimers, whether in preaching, teaching or pastoring, first listen intently within the culture in which both they and their prospective hearers are immersed. The message is both offered and at the same time discerned. By contrast propagandists are so preoccupied with their message that they ignore the hearers and the cultural conditioning of the words which they speak. While this assurance may appeal to some people and draw them to follow the propagandist, for most it is not ultimately convincing.

This observation leads us finally to note that congruity is needed between what is being taught and the methods of teaching. In the theological education of the ordinand as pastor the mode of interpretative ministry and the mode of learning both require the same stance: telling stories, hearing, listening, and responding. For such a role the predominant educational pattern will, therefore, be one of seminars and group activity, in which the structure of the programme and its content not only cohere but also interweave.

Notes

1. See above pp. 8–9.

2. Carr, *The Priestlike Task*, p. 50.

3. This study would not be purely of media output. Such writing as, for example, Bernice Martin's *A Sociology of Contemporary Cultural Change* (1981) would be apposite.

4. Robin Gill, *A Textbook of Christian Ethics* (Edinburgh, T. & T. Clark, 1988), p. 23.

5. John Foskett and David Lyall, *Helping the Helpers: Supervision and Pastoral Care* (London, SPCK, 1988), p. 49.

6. Carr, *The Pastor as Theologian*.

7. Bernice Martin, *Sociology*, p. 28.

11 SPIRITUAL FORMATION

'Formation' used to be distinctively a Roman Catholic term. Today, however, it permeates discussions on ministry, since it describes a field of study which is recognized as common to all ministerial training. It connects two significant topics in contemporary church life. First, there is that area of religious experience which is loosely called 'spirituality'. This imprecise word describes the heart of religious activity. And, while primarily personal, it also has connections with the institutional life of the Churches. People rightly look to Churches, as well as their ministers, as places where prayer is offered and some sort of holiness can be expected. Second, there is the matter of forming the nature of people for the distinctive role of the minister or priest. And high on any list of required characteristics would be that he or she be a prayerful person with spiritual depth.

A clear, recent statement on this comes from *Ministry and Mission: Proposals for a National Policy for Lifelong Priestly Formation*. The Roman Catholic bishops of England and Wales develop the Decree on Priestly Formation from the Second Vatican Council:

> Formation as one of Christ's ministers must thus be a process of 'putting on Christ'. It must concentrate on the development of each student who must grow to a Christ-like maturity. The programme of formation must be one of personal formation and not simply the acquisition of skills and knowledge. There are three dimensions to this personal growth: human, Christian and priestly.[1]

This could now be written, *mutatis mutandis*, about ministerial training in any Church. The aim of this aspect of training is to encourage, indeed to ensure, the minister's spiritual growth. This is sometimes confused with personal, or psychological growth, and the quest for spiritual formation may drift towards therapy. Occasionally this may be needed. But spiritual formation is an educational function, by which we relate to appropriate personal growth to the professional 'growth' (or a deepening grasp of role) required in the minister.

Robert Leavitt has pointed out how in the Roman Catholic Church the identity of the priest as cultic leader and as teacher has declined since the Second Vatican Council.[2] This has partly followed the intention of those ministerial ideals which predominated in the 1970s and partly been an effect of their being implemented. During that period the idea of the minister as 'pastor', someone given in service to people, became increasingly popular. However, the freedom which the role of priest (or for that matter, minister) provided, gave clergy a basis from which to become counsellors and social workers, whether as ministers in their parishes or as professionals after leaving the Churches' ministry. Most acquired some psychological skills, but in so doing both their training and their experience of ministry became overloaded. What had previously been considered the basic requirements of ministry with the Christian community became less prominent.

Leavitt expounds this in terms of the role of the priest as leader and co-ordinator of the gifts which are to be found in the Christian community. But even if we give the public role more emphasis by stressing that the minister is not only the servant but also a representative of the Christian community, the result is the same: a demand that he or she should possess and demonstrate spiritual depth and vision.

Leavitt describes this vision as

> the spiritual art of fashioning new metaphors of faith that are both faithful to divine revelation and practically meaningful for this group of Christians. The priest does this by simultaneous attention to God's Word and our human experience and by the continuing effort to put into new words what both teach us.[3]

A key point arises from this discussion. There is a profound link between the minister's spirituality — what makes him or her continue as a Christian — and his or her public presentation. This is not a matter of the 'inside' being correctly conveyed to the 'outside'. That is, as we have already noted, a simplistic and deficient view of communication. Prayerfulness and spiritual depth are as much the result of engagement with people in the role of minister as of any private disposition towards holiness.

BROADCASTING AND SPIRITUAL FORMATION

Putting this aspect of ministerial development specifically in relation to broadcasting and the media we are brought face to face with the question of meanings or the varieties of interpretations of experiences which are unique for the person experiencing them but common enough to undergo comparison and so become the material of teaching. And this illumination may suggest to us one way of reflecting on the controversial but important topic of the sacramental nature of ministry. Robert White, another Catholic writer, has taken Leavitt's reflections and developed them in this direction. He then concludes:

> If the preparation of the priest in the past meant providing a fund of sound doctrine with which to give more formal guidance to people already filled with catholic culture, today the preparation of the priest must stress a *deep personal experience* of the saving action of Christ and a cultivated sensitivity to the cultural symbols of a given community. In our contemporary mass-mediated culture, this means above all a sensitivity to the symbols, myths and folk-tale plots of the mass media which are such an important source of the religious imagination today. [italics mine][4]

The italics direct attention to the question of the place of spirituality in formation. The phrase describes what Protestants might call 'a conversion experience'. Most Churches increasingly recognize that such an experience, whether of conversion to Christian faith or of vocation to ordained ministry, does not occur once and for all. There is a continuing and lifelong dimension to spiritual formation, which, if it is to be sustained, has to be structured and ordered.

The second point to note is White's reference to 'imagination'. We have repeatedly commented on how vital this topic is in contemporary theological education. Now we discover its potential as an integrating factor, which links the teaching and preaching of the gospel with the inner experiencing of it. Imagination provides a perspective on personal growth and religious maturity, and it is one which is affected by the existence of the modern media.

Ministerial training cannot proceed without attention to spiritual formation in its widest sense and few, if any, courses ignore it. Nevertheless students report that it often feels like a disconnected part of their programme. Vague notions of 'spirituality' can become a refuge from the harder questions of learning and the practice of ministry. Yet to leave spiritual formation to the students alone on the grounds that it is a private matter between them and, say, their tutor or spiritual director, denies a key aspect of the minister's spirituality: his or her spiritual life is public.

The emphasis on signs and symbols in communication theory is useful in clarifying this aspect of the minister's role. They remind us of the serendipitous and haphazard nature of religious experience and its communication. In the field of prayer and spirituality ministers frequently discover a gap between their intentions and the outcome. It is as if the congruence of a set of symbols—priest, minister, church, cross, incense, etc.—and wistful intention in prayer creates an arena in which the unexpected may happen. To prepare men and women for confidence in such ministry requires that spiritual formation should be a core subject in the programme of theological education.

We may examine this on two levels. First, there is ritual. Public praying, for instance, is one such activity, as is any liturgical rite. Archetypal themes seem to permeate human life. They do not themselves disappear, even when the means by which they are expressed change. An essential clarification of communication is to distinguish between transmission and ritual. In transmission we are concerned with space. The aim of such communication is to convey or transport a message, and the outcome is exploration of where power lies and how the politics of the activity are to be interpreted. Ritual communication, by contrast, is more concerned with time, as symbols are used to provide some sense of order and community on the archetypal experiences of men and women.

We earlier noticed the experience of the participants in the Project that, when they began to reflect consciously on the media world which they inhabit, they found themselves pressed further to consider their inner life. The outer/inner distinction, while not dissolved, was nevertheless discovered to be less absolute than might have been thought. This issue is the essence of spiritual formation around the question of meaning. For ministers have to discover how to live publicly (that is, under scrutiny by others) what they experience most privately.

The connection between these two aspects of spirituality is through symbols, and especially through a deeper and developing awareness of two points. First, ministers are themselves symbols and function as such. Their spiritual activity, therefore, does not consist solely of their own spiritual sustenance and actions. Interaction between oneself and God and between oneself-in-role (which includes the part of that role which is assigned through the expectations of others) and God, bring about development in spiritual depth. Second, the world of available symbols has been (and is still being) greatly enlarged by the prevalence of the mass media. If ministers are not alert to these two points, their spirituality and that of the Churches will possibly become isolated from the meaning-bearing media in our society and thus seem increasingly problematic and irrelevant rather than a lively and natural point of interpretation in a complex world.

Gregor Goethals has explored some of these issues with particular reference to people's need for heroes and new icons and for some sense of adventure in their humdrum existence.

> Until institutional religion can excite *the serious play of the soul* and evoke the fullness of human passion, television will nurture our illusions of heroism and self-transcendence.[5]

The phrase 'serious play of the soul' is an apt description of prayer and the spiritual life. It is also another way of describing liturgy, the serious play or drama of the symbolic representation of God, human life and their intersection. Attention to the media in this context is potentially valuable in integrating personal spirituality and liturgical function in a process of genuine formation or integrated learning.

The second level of reflection, however, is more practical. Spiritual formation is concerned with meanings to all aspects of life: how an object can become a means to deeper knowledge of God; how a text can become a means to further the pilgrimage; how a hymn can lift the soul to heaven. These and similar enquiries are all important for ordinands and those to whom they will in due course minister. They are also all questions of communications.

It may perhaps be too easy to be too highbrow here. But an excessively vulgar touch will also be flawed. For, as the media consistently demonstrate, however trivial something may seem, when it is made the focus for reflection, it automatically raises the question of meaning. One danger, however, is that the immediacy of the media may tend to isolate us inadvertently in a culturally limited time-frame. Dean Inge's warning that those who marry the spirit of the age will be widowed in the next is apposite. Those who are expected to handle questions of ultimate meaning and issues of eternity cannot be constrained by the activity of the moment.

LITERARY/ARTS STUDIES AND SPIRITUAL FORMATION

If we are to think about images and icons, we need to be confident in the field of imagination and creativity—that is, the arts. It is, incidentally, noteworthy that much of the most intriguing output in the media comes about when these two worlds, literature and art, are joined. For instance, programmes of poetry and music on the radio or words and pictures on the television prove powerfully evocative and stimulating to the imagination, not least in programmes from the religious broadcasting departments. Christian ministers, of whatever Church, stand in a cultural tradition. It is appropriate, therefore, that they should know something about it. But in addition, through even a minimum acquaintance with that tradition and with the contemporary arts, they could begin to engage creatively with the opportunities for prayer and liturgy which are presented to them in their day-to-day ministry.

The specific contribution of literary studies to spiritual formation comes through art and poetry. Iconography, in the wide sense, is part of the rich spiritual tradition of the Church. Icons portray people, saints, martyrs and those to be emulated, just as today's media focus on the human dimensions to stories. Learning of this sort is not something to be acquired so that it may subsequently be given to a congregation. It is rather a soul-nourishing dimension to life. Those ministers who are imbued with it will be more profound people and so more explorable pastors and teachers. Poetry, which already plays a large part in

137

the life of the Church through the Psalms, the Old Testament and hymns, would also be given careful attention. In the end, however, all these themes point to the central question for all Christians: When we pray to God (the Other and the unknown), what sort of communication is taking place? Confidence with the question, whatever the response, is essential for ministers.

COMMUNICATION THEORY AND SPIRITUAL FORMATION

There is little that communications' studies contribute directly to spiritual formation, except perhaps an earthing function to philosophical examination of the nature of faith and prayer. One field, however, which is prominent in contemporary communications' research is significant: the question of culture. Thinking about, as well as the practice of, spirituality raises the critical relationship between the Christian Church and any prevailing culture.

In approaching this topic writers often employ the categories outlined by Richard Niebuhr. For present purposes we need only list them: (1) Christ against culture, a simple rejection of the world; (2) Christ of culture, as the Church reflects the values of the prevailing culture; (3) Christ above culture, as the belief is that Christ draws society to a level higher than human aspirations; (4) Christ and culture in paradox, the Lutheran position according to which we live in a permanent but hopeful tension between the demands of Christ and the demands of the culture; and (5) Christ the transformer of culture, which sees culture as transmitting fallen human nature and the Church as converting people within that setting, so that they shine as lights in the world.[6]

This is a useful analysis, although at no time in Christian experience have these attitudes been compartmentalized. Most Christians have lived, and still do, in a mixture of positions. But this clarification points us to another key issue concerning spiritual formation, namely that it is less a matter of analytical skill or knowledge than of discernment. This is a topic which directly connects with our media-saturated environment and so brings communications' studies and spiritual formation together. James McDonnell comments:

Discernment, like prayer, requires a measure of silence and solitude in our life . . . Disengagement every now and then from the noise of the media provides precious moments in which to listen to God and to examine how far we are creative and free in our media use.[7]

He goes on to discuss the notion of imaginative use of the media:

In the effort of hearing what it is others are saying or trying to say (as opposed to what they seem to say), we make ourselves vulnerable. We may find ourselves touched more deeply by our encounters with people through the media as well as by direct personal encounter. The stories of war and famine we hear on the news may become more real to us; we may feel more deeply about people and events we know only through the television, radio or newspaper. We may discover that programmes and music that once were so much background now have the power to engage our attention and move our hearts. In short, we may discover that 'imaginative listening' is not far removed from the contemplative spirit.[8]

This connection between everyday activity—in this case viewing and listening—and prayer is exactly what classical spiritual teachers have emphasized. It may be, too, that two aspects to 'discernment' might be creatively brought together. There is, on the one hand, discernment as an expression of wisdom and judgement. This is what training programmes like that in Television Awareness have proposed. On the other hand, there is discernment in the sense of perceiving the trails of God through this world. Competence in both of these roles, educator and spiritual guide, is required of ministers.

The idea of discernment within the cultural framework, to which attention is drawn by the media, directs students to three issues: their role as discerner, teacher, and spiritual director; their role as exemplars of discernment and spirituality; and the critical engagement with its culture, which constitutes the nature of the Church of which they are to be ministers.

One of the marks of contemporary theological education is the paucity of preparation for ministers to be spiritual guides or directors to the members of their congregations. Surveys of preaching, for instance, expose the fact that sermons are so general that people are unsure about what is being said. Yet every preacher also knows that exceptional specificity in the pulpit can either produce a debilitating dependency on the preacher, who is heard uncritically, or a failure to communicate clearly what is intended.

For this reason among others adult education is today increasingly attempted in small face-to-face groups. But even here the content is often strangely irrelevant. Some, for instance, are Bible study groups, in which either the minister (as the 'trained' person) or a written course dominates. Others devote themselves to approaches derived from other cultures, especially places where the Church is believed to be more lively or successful than in the United Kingdom. Yet if today's major cultural phenomenon is the mass media, it would seem sensible primarily to relate the learning of Christian people to the issues which are raised by engagement with that culture.

Preoccupation with media tends itself to be culturally conditioned. The main American Churches, for instance, are concerned with tele-evangelists; Third World Churches fear cultural imperialism; the mainland Europeans philosophize about communications; while the British pursue their customary pragmatism. Yet from all this ideas are emerging which may prove useful for theological education.

For example, in the USA, where television in particular has been long a significant factor in everyday cultural life, the Media Action Research Center has produced a programme called *Television Awareness Training* (T–A–T).

> T–A–T is a curriculum which helps persons become more aware of the messages and influence of the television experience, more creative in the use of TV, and work for a television system that better serves the needs of the public. The curriculum focuses on television as our most common experience, something much more than an advertising or entertainment medium, a major transmitter of culture, a shaper of values, setter of lifestyles, a conditioner of the way we think, believe, and feel. Since so much of what television portrays of our culture is antithetical to human values, the course of study stresses the need of making viewing an intentional and evaluative experience.[9]

Such an approach could be a useful contribution to any programme of theological education. We are not here thinking of skills (in this case, educational skills) that ministers might acquire. The primary reason for this suggestion is that through such critical attention both to the media and to themselves, students will learn about the context of their ministry at the same time as they will also reflect on their own spiritual formation.

The question, 'How is television influencing people?', cannot be asked without its also becoming, 'How am I interacting with television?' That question makes the issue self-reflective, and for the religious person any such reflection is spiritually forming. For it directs the students' mind to themselves and their culture—that is, the basic interaction of all Christian ministry. And it also emphasizes that this encounter occurs both outside and within oneself. Students then have consciously to become aware of themselves both as inhabitants of a general cultural context and as Christian believers seeking to move forward on a spiritual pilgrimage.

The point at which such learning links with communication theory is both obvious and complex. In the spiritual life, especially prayer, the idea of communication is central. The difficulty arises when we ask what sort of communication occurs between people and God. The philosophical aspect to the question will receive attention in a programme of theological education. But equally important will be the idea of artistic communication. One outcome of this we may confidently expect would be better informed behaviour, a larger sensitivity to God, and greater awareness of others. Unsurprisingly these three stances correspond to the traditional forms of prayer: meditation (attention to oneself), contemplation (attention to God) and intercession (concern for one's neighbour). Profound illumination of the process of spiritual formation will derive from serious attention to the media.

Notes

1. op. cit., p. 284.

2. Robert J. Leavitt, 'Priesthood and Seminary', *Seminaries in Dialogue*, NCEA, Washington DC, (1983), pp. 15ff, cited by Robert A. White, 'The New Communications Emerging in the Church', *The Way* 57 Supplement (1986), pp. 4ff.

3. Leavitt, 'Priesthood', p. 17.

4. White, 'New Communications', p. 24.

5. Goethals, *TV Ritual*, p. 143.

6. H. Richard Niebuhr, *Christ and Culture* (New York, Harper Row, 1951).

7. James McDonnell, 'Christian Discernment in a Mass-Mediated Culture', *The Way* 57 Supplement (1986), p. 38.

8. McDonnell, 'Christian Discernment', p. 42.

9. Ben Logan, ed., *Television Awareness Training; The Viewer's Guide for Family and Community* (Abingdon/Nashville, MARC, 1979), p. 269.

12 LEADERSHIP AND SOCIAL SKILL

So far in this discussion the Church has been chiefly considered in general terms within its setting and the roles of the ordained minister examined. But it is also important that ministers should gain some sense of the institutional Church which they serve and the leadership which it will demand of them. Idealized Churches do not exist.

Whatever view of ministry prevails, the assumption which ministers find themselves facing is that they are leaders. They may work dictatorially or collaboratively, and probably at various points on that continuum, but they are still expected to lead. The area covered, therefore, in this fourth component of the syllabus is concerned with activities and functioning of the local church as unit, within which the ordained minister will be expected to take some leadership role.

It might appear that the media have little to contribute to the study of the Church's organization and leadership within it. No doubt at a stretch links can be discerned, but these are not obvious. Nevertheless learning about leadership is important for ministers, not least because it assists them to reflect upon the Church as an organization or institution and their place and function within it.

This chapter, therefore, will be more brief than the preceding three, not because the topic is unimportant but because the direct impact of media and communications' studies is less. The chief input, as will be seen from the schematic presentation, is through the broadcasting dimension.

BROADCASTING, LEADERSHIP AND SOCIAL SKILL

The media are voracious. They always need more material and seek it out. The aggressive side of this activity is sometimes noticed and deplored. But much more of the time is spent

143

finding news (especially by the local media) and reporting it. This is a genuine service. However, the media also have their own standards of what is reportable or presentable, and it is usually when these conflict with the expectations of those providing the stories that anger is aroused. Yet a moment's reflection reminds us that no one controls their own presentation. In any interpersonal or intergroup activity images are generated which have a profound effect on assumptions about oneself and others. The media question of what is reportable and how it is to be presented then ceases to be a matter of technical skill alone. Attention to such study may also bring the student to thinking about images of the Church which are based upon people's perceptions rather than *a priori* ideals.

The broadcasting dimension to this aspect of the syllabus, therefore, primarily offers a corrective to the usual approach to the study of ecclesiology. It roots explorations of models of the Church in the question of how those models arise through interaction between those holding beliefs and those to whom, or among whom, they are presented.

There is a tendency for theological teachers and students alike to become grandiose about the Church. Working from texts, they construct models of the Church which bear scant relation to actual context. The behavioural reasons for this are obvious: the teacher may be working out some frustration with himself or the Church, without the controlling effect of an existent (and critical) congregation. The student inevitably lacks the experience of projections onto the authorized minister. There ensues, therefore, elaborate discussion of what might be and what theoretically is the case. Such mind-enlarging study is not to be despised, but its limitations are noticeable, especially when we employ a media perspective on this training. Models need both theological criticism and the test of how presentable they are. Images alone are not enough; the communication of ideas is also essential.

The connection of this study with two other aspects of the syllabus may be noted. First, different models of the Church imply different approaches to liturgy. Study of this area would enable ministers to discover the unconscious discontinuities that are often found in the experience of church life. One model of the Church is adumbrated, while an alternative is symbolically expressed. Ministers are constantly caught in this dilemma. In order to live and work with it they need instinctively to be able to ask why this is happening and what theological interpretation of the phenomenon might be possible. Too easily the 'high' theologies of the Church in practice give place to casual behavioural interpretations of actual church life. Second, preaching, in the wide sense used earlier, needs to be congruent in style to the model of Church that is being emphasized both liturgically and structurally.

Such points are obvious. The question arises for most teachers, however, as to how they are to be addressed. If, however, a media perspective—in this instance, what is reportable—is adopted towards what is experienced, these questions may become clearer. For the media offer a third term by which to connect the other two and to examine each. Theoretically, for example, it is clear that there is an intimate connection between ecclesiology, liturgy and homiletics. But how is a programme of theological education to make this sufficiently real for students and teachers alike for them to study it? To this problem use of the media may provide the beginnings of a solution.

COMMUNICATION THEORY, LEADERSHIP AND SOCIAL SKILL

When we turn to training in leadership, a number of points of useful interest may be found in communication theory. Most of these have already been mentioned and will not be repeated. Generally modern communications' studies make use of the range of human sciences, especially sociology and psychology. But the integration of human sciences and theological study remains elusive.

It would be foolish to suggest that the use of communications' studies provides the solution to this difficulty. But if we are right that this orientation in theological education will have benefits in application and clarification, then it seems that this may be another way in which to ground psychological and sociological learning in the overall course. For these disciplines consistently draw attention to the two keys of task—what we are about, and role—what is an individual's functional place within that task. Specifically, there is no way in which the course can be pursued without the student having to consider the socio-cultural relations of language and some of the issues of perception and interactive behaviour, as well as the nature of institutions and the meanings that they carry.

For the authorized minister there is no escape from the expectations focused in him or her. The Church today is taking a variety of forms and is likely to be a changing organization. Its ministers, therefore, have to be flexible enough to be able to discern these expectations and interpret them in relation to the Church's task. Much of this will be done locally in the congregation. But it may be overlooked, not least in courses of theological education, that they will also be expected to offer similar leadership in the wider Church through councils and synods. Some conception of the Church as organization and institution is essential, and this may better be derived from media presentations of the Church as perceived by others and interpreted with reference to sociological and psychological study than through traditional ecclesiology.

CONCLUSION

There was, during the heyday of the Biblical Theology movement, much play with the two notions of 'Word' and 'words'. The hermeneutical question of how the living Christ was to be made present through human words was carefully considered, even as church attendance (and consequently the number of people hearing sermons) was declining. Already communication was a greater problem than many had realized.

Today, as we have seen, the issues facing the Churches' ministers have become more complex and acute. By their existence the modern mass media, especially television, arouse anxiety. 'Revolution' is frequently used in writings on the subject, both by those largely in favour of recent developments and by those against. Whatever one's instinctive feeling, one thing is certain: the media are not a temporary aberration. They are here to stay and their pervasive influence, however we determine that, will continue to increase.

I have suggested that when viewed as a cultural phenomenon, the media can be approached critically but also positively. Much needs to be done in detail. The Project out of which this work began, continues in its aim to produce detailed curricula material for educators. Programmes like Television Awareness Training will continue. Commissions will continue to consider and report on the use of the media by religion. All these and similar efforts need encouraging.

For Christian ministers, however, whether ordained or lay, in post or in training, alertness to the media as providing the context within which their everyday ministry is exercised has become an urgent concern. The great problems are important, but the form and content of the Christian gospel—that which has any impact on the lives of men and women—is a more immediate issue. The delusion that it is sufficient to acquire skills in communications must be resisted. The reality of the world which the Churches' ministers have to interpret with the light of the gospel must be acknowledged. And for this task in this generation careful attention to the media and their significance is no longer an option but a requirement.

BIBLIOGRAPHY

Armstrong, Peter, 'Television as a Medium for Theology', in Peter Eaton, ed., *The Trial of Faith*. Worthing, Churchman Publishing, 1988.

Arthur, Christopher J., *In the Hall of Mirrors: Problems of Commitment in a Religiously Plural World*. Oxford, Mowbray, 1986.

Arthur, Christopher J., 'Television, Transcendence and Religious Education', *Farmington Occasional Paper 27*. Oxford, Farmington Institute for Christian Studies, 1987.

Berger, Peter, *A Rumour of Angels: Modern Society and the Rediscovery of the Supernatural*. Harmondsworth, Penguin, 1971.

Bocock, Robert J., *Ritual in Industrial Society*. London, George Allen and Unwin, 1974.

Brooks, R. T., *Communicating Conviction*. London, Epworth, 1983.

Carr, Wesley, 'Working with Dependency and Remaining Sane', in Giles Ecclestone, ed., *The Parish Church?*. London, Mowbray, 1988.

Carr, Wesley, *The Priestlike Task*. London, SPCK, 1985.

Carr, Wesley, *Brief Encounters: Pastoral Ministry through the Occasional Offices*. London, SPCK, 1985.

Carr, Wesley, *The Pastor as Theologian: The Integration of Pastoral Ministry, Theology and Discipleship*. London, SPCK, 1989.

Comstock, G., ed., *Public Communication and Behavior*, vol. 1. Orlando, Academic Press, 1986.

Conrad, Peter, *Television, the Medium and its Manners*. London, Routledge and Kegan Paul, 1982.

Corner, John, and Hawthorn, Jeremy, eds, *Communication Studies*. London, Edward Arnold, 2nd ed. 1985.

Curran, James, 'Communications, Power and Social Order', in Michael Gurevitch, Tony Bennett, James Curran and Janet Woollacott, eds, *Culture, Society and the Media*. London, Methuen, 1982.

Dulles, Avery, 'The Church is Communications', *US Catholic Documentary Service*, 1971. New York, US Catholic Conference.

Elvy, Peter, *Buying Time*. Southend-on-Sea, McCrimmon, 1987.

Evans, Christopher, *Explorations in Theology 2*. London, SCM Press, 1977.

Fiske, John, *Television Culture*. London, Methuen, 1987.

Fore, William F., *Television and Religion*. Minneapolis, Augsburg Publishing, 1987.

Foskett, John, and Lyall, David, *Helping the Helpers: Supervision and Pastoral Care*. London, SPCK, 1988.

Gill, Robin, *A Textbook of Christian Ethics*. Edinburgh, T. and T. Clark, 1988.

Goethals, Gregor, *The TV Ritual: Worship at the Video Altar*. Boston, Beacon Press, 1981.

Habgood, John, *Church and Nation in a Secular Age*. London, Darton, Longman and Todd, 1983.

Handy, Charles, *The Age of Unreason*. London, Hutchinson, 1989.

Hay, David, *Exploring Inner Space*. Harmondsworth, Penguin, 1982.

Hiesburger, Jean Marie, 'The Ultimate Challenge to Religious Education'. *Religious Education* 76 (1981).

Hodgson, Leonard, *For Faith and Freedom*. London, Darton, Longman and Todd, 2nd ed. 1968.

Hoover, Stewart M., *Mass Media Religion: The Social Sources of the Electronic Church*. Newbury Park, California, Sage, 1988.

Horsfield, Peter, 'Religious Dimensions of Television's Uses and Content'. *Colloquium* 17 (1985).

Hull, John, *What Prevents Adult Christians from Learning?* London, SCM Press, 1985.

Katz, Elihu, and Dayan, Daniel, 'Media Events: On the Experience of Not being There'. *Religion* 15 (1983).

Leach, Edmund, *Culture and Communication: The Logic by which Symbols are Connected*. Cambridge, CUP, 1976.

Leavitt, Robert J., 'Priesthood and Seminary', in *Seminaries in Dialogue*. NCEA, Washington DC, 1983.

Lienemann-Perrin, Christine, *Training for Relevant Ministry: A Study of the Work of the Theological Education Fund*. Madras, The Christian Literature Society, 1981.

Logan, Ben, ed., *Television Awareness Training: The Viewer's Guide for Family and Community*. Abingdon/Nashville, MARC, 1979.

Martin, Bernice, *A Sociology of Contemporary Cultural Change*. Oxford, Blackwell, 1981.

McDonnell, James, 'Christian Discernment in a Mass-Mediated Culture'. *The Way* 57 Supplement (1986).

McQuail, Denis, 'The influence and effects of mass media', in James Curran, Michael Gurevitch and Janet Woollacott, eds, *Mass Communication and Society*. London, Edward Arnold, 1977.

Modell, Arthur, *Psychoanalysis in a New Context*. New York, International Universities Press, 1985.

Morley, David and Whitaker, Brian, eds, *The Press, Radio and Television*. London, Commedia, n.d.

Morris, Colin, *God in a Box*. London, Hodder and Stoughton, 1984.

Muggeridge, Malcolm, *Christ and the Media*. London, Hodder and Stoughton, 1977.

Niebuhr, H. Richard, *Christ and Culture*. New York, Harper Row, 1951.

Pannenberg, Wolfhart, *Anthropology in a Theological Perspective*. Edinburgh, T. and T. Clark, 1985.

Parker, Stanley, *The Future of Work and Leisure*. London, McGibbon and Kee, 1971.

Postman, Neil, *Amusing Ourselves to Death*. London, Methuen, 1986.

Real, Michael, *Mass Mediated Culture*. Englewood-Cliffs, Prentice-Hall, 1977.

Reed, Bruce, *The Dynamics of Religion*. London, Darton, Longman and Todd, 1978.

Robinson, Edward, and Jackson, Michael, *Religious Values at Sixteen Plus*. Oxford, Alister Hardy Research Centre, 1987.

Shapiro, Edward R. and Carr, Wesley, 'Disguised Countertransference in Institutions'. *Psychiatry* 59 (1987).

Shapiro, Edward R., and Carr, Wesley, *Lost in Familiar Places: The Interpretation of Experience from Family to Society*. Princeton and London, Yale UP, 1991.

Thiselton, Anthony, *The Two Horizons*. Exeter, Paternoster, 1980.

Turner, Victor, *The Ritual Process*. London, Routledge and Kegan Paul, 1969.

White, Robert A., 'The New Communications Emerging in the Church'. *The Way* 57 Supplement (1986).

White, Robert A., 'Formation for Priestly Ministry in a Mass-Mediated Culture'. *Seminarius* 4.

Winnicott, Donald W., *The Maturational Process and the Facilitating Environment*. London, Hogarth Press, 1965.

Winnicott, Donald W., 'The Theory of the Parent-Infant Relationship'. *The International Journal of Psycho-Analysis* 41 (1960).

Wolfe, Kenneth M., *The Churches and the British Broadcasting Corporation, 1922–1956*. London, SCM Press, 1984.

Index